Celebrating the Coretta Scott King Awards

Awards

■ 101 ■
Ideas & Activities

Nancy J. Polette

Alleyside Press

Fort Atkinson, Wisconsin

Published by Alleyside Press,
an imprint of Highsmith Press LLC
Highsmith Press
W5527 Highway 106
P.O. Box 800
Fort Atkinson, Wisconsin 53538-0800
1-800-558-2110

The paper used in this publication meets the minimum requirements of
American National Standard for Information Science - Permanence of
Paper for Printed Library Material. ANSI/NISO Z39.48-1992.

Contents

Introduction

Celebrating the Coretta Scott King Awards gives both the information and ready-to-use activities needed for the busy teacher or librarian who wants to share these outstanding books with children. The winning titles chosen for inclusion are those that can be shared in one class session or library story time. The activities are designed to meet the diverse needs of school and public librarians and teachers.

For each featured winner a brief plot summary and author/illustrator biographical information is provided. This is accompanied by poetry, art, singing, craft, writing and/or research activities. Also accompanying each book is an annotated list of titles with similar themes. An Internet activity is included as a resource for the teacher or librarian. Many of the Internet activities can be printed out and used by children in computer labs in the school or by an individual child on the library or home computer.

Among the many craft activities are making "amazing apples" following the sharing of the New York City (Big Apple) story of *Tar Beach*; designing the monster Melissa might have seen in the chicken coop from *The Dark Thirty*; filling a basket with "Talking Eggs"; creating the seasons after hearing *The Creation* and many more.

Research and writing activities are included for use in the classroom to build comprehension, writing and research skills that result in products in which children can take pride.

Books and activities can also be combined for theme programs or studies. Suggestions include:

A Folktale Fest
Beat the Story-Drum, Pum-Pum; Her Stories: African American Folktales; The People Could Fly

Spunky Heroines
Aida; Mirandy and Brother Wind; Mufaro's Beautiful Daughters

Great African Americans
Cornrows; The Friendship; Minty: A Story of Young Harriet Tubman

African American Children Today
Justin and the Best Biscuits in the World; Nathaniel Talking; My Mama Needs Me

The Coretta Scott King Award is given annually by the Social Responsibilities Round Table of the American Library Association to an African American author and an African American illustrator for outstanding inspirational and educational contributions to literature for children. The idea for the award came from school librarians Glyndon Greer and Mabel McKissack who first proposed it in 1969. In 1982 the award became an official award of the Social Responsibilities Round Table of the American Library Association.

Celebrating the Coretta Scott King Awards will help librarians and teachers to truly celebrate with children these outstanding books in a variety of ways. These are titles that should become a part of every child's literary legacy and this book will help make this goal a reality.

Africa Dream

Written by Eloise Greenfield, Illustrated by Carole Byard
1978 Author Award Winner

About the Book

A young child dreams of visiting long ago Africa, crossing an ocean in "one smooth jump." The animals are waiting, elephants, zebras, and camels. The child visits a market place and sees ancient civilizations with their tall stone buildings. Riding on a donkey through crowds of people the child sees many diverse faces. The dream continues, taking the child to a long ago grandfather's village where mango seeds are planted and dances are performed to the beat of drums. Finally the child returns home, still dreaming of being rocked to sleep by a "long-ago grandma." *(John Day, 1977. 32 pp. Reading Level: 3.0)*

About the Author

Eloise Greenfield is the author of more than twenty books for children. Her biographies, fiction and poetry have received numerous awards for excellence including the first Carter G. Woodson Award, the Jane Addams Children's Book Award and the Hope S. Dean Award for her body of work. Ms. Greenfield has taught creative writing in Washington, D.C., schools as an artist-in-education for the D.C. Commission on the Arts and Humanities. She was born in North Carolina but has spent most of her life in Washington, D.C.

About the Illustrator

Carole Byard has traveled to Africa several times in making a loving study of African life and culture. She was born in New Jersey and showed her talent as an artist at a very early age. She attended Fleischer Art Memorial and the Phoenix School of Design. She worked as a teacher of art and was a founding member of the Black Artists Guild. She served as a delegate to an international black arts conference in Nigeria and her visit there is reflected in many of her illustrations.

Before Reading Activity

Five Senses Group Poem

Using the handout on page 9, have the children create a five senses group poem about what they may meet if they dreamed about Africa.

After Reading Activities

Questions to Think About

After reading *Africa Dream,* ask the children to think about the following questions and share their answers.

1. What parts of the dream do you believe were true?

2. Were there really tall buildings in ancient Africa? How can you find out?

3. What other African animals can you name that the child might have seen?

4. Would you like to visit Africa? Why or why not?

Make an Animal Fact/Fiction Book

For this fun way to report on animals, have each child make a book about an animal of their choice. On one page of a spread, have them draw a picture and write a true or false statement about the animal. On the other page of the spread, have them tell if the statement is true or false and add a little more about the subject. When the books are finished, share them with the group. Hold up the page with the true or false statement and have the group guess if it is fact or fiction.

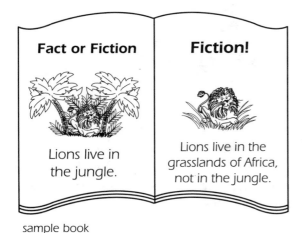

Fact or Fiction

Lions live in the jungle.

Fiction!

Lions live in the grasslands of Africa, not in the jungle.

sample book

African Animal Acrostic Poem

Have the children write an acrostic poem about an animal. Give them a sample like the one below.

L ions live in Africa.

I n tall grasses.

O ne lion can move very quietly.

N anny goats are a lion's favorite meal.

Foot Poem

Copy the handout on page 10 and have each child write a Foot Poem.

African Dancing Mask

Using the pattern on page 11, create individual dancing masks.

Additional Reading

More About Africa

Onyefulu, Ifeoma. *A Is for Africa.* Dutton. 1993. 32 pp. RL: 2.0. An alphabet book illustrated with photographs taken in Nigeria.

Arnold, Caroline. *African Animals.* William Morrow, 1997. 32 pp. RL: 2.0. Full-color photographs of African wildlife in its native environment.

Kroll, Virginia. *Africa Brothers and Sisters.* Simon & Schuster, 1993. 32 pp. RL: 2.0. An American boy learns about his African brothers and sisters and their shared heritage.

Alderman, Daniel A. *Africa Calling.* Whispering Coyote Press, 1996. 32 pp. RL: 3.0. A girl imagines herself in Africa with lions, monkeys, rhinos, zebras and other animals.

Hoffman, Mary. *Boundless Grace.* Dial Books, 1995. 32 pp. RL: 2.0. While visiting her father in Africa, Grace learns about another culture and that even divided families can be loving.

Five Senses Poem

Places are often described using the five senses. Below is a sample poem that is written using all five senses.

> A meadow can be green or gold.
> It sounds like ladies' skirts swishing in the breeze,
> It tastes like fresh baked bread.
> It smells like fresh cut hay.
> It makes you feel like running through the tall grasses.

What colors, sounds, tastes, smells, sights and feelings do think you might meet if you dreamed about Africa? Share ideas to create the five senses poem below.

Line 1 Tell what colors you will see
Line 2 Tell what it sounds like
Line 3 Tell what it tastes like
Line 4 Tell what it smells like
Line 5 Tell what it looks like
Line 6 Tell how it makes you feel

Africa is the color of _____

It sounds like _____

It tastes like _____

It smells like _____

It looks like _____

It makes you feel like _____

After reading *Africa Dream*, create another Five Senses Poem. What new sights, sounds, colors and smells will you add?

Foot Poem

Follow this pattern below to write a "Foot" poem about an animal.

If I had the feet of a <u>rhino,</u>
I'd <u>have an odd number of toes on each foot,</u>
And <u>I'd have weak eyesight, but good hearing and a strong sense of smell,</u>
But I wouldn't <u>be very active at night</u>
Because <u>armadillos</u> do that.

Basic model:

If I had the feet of _____,

I'd _____,

And I'd _____,

But I wouldn't _____

because _____ do that.

Draw a picture of your feet below:

African Dancing Mask

Dance was very important to many African tribes. They would dance when a child was born, when someone died, to gain courage for battle, to celebrate a victory, to drive away evil spirits, to bring rain, to make crops grow and to imitate the movement of animals or fish they wished to bring home.

Create an African dancing mask using the pattern below. Tell what the purpose of your mask is.

See pictures of other African masks on the Internet at this website:

The Art of the African Mask
http://cti.itc.virginia.edu/~bcr/African_Mask.html

Aida

Illustrated by Leo & Diane Dillon, Told by Leontyne Price
1991 Illustrator Award Winner

About the Book

Aida is a royal princess of the African nation of Ethiopia. The proud and beautiful girl loves her father and her country above all else. When she is captured by Egyptian soldiers, she is made a slave to the daughter of the Pharaoh, Amneris. Aida hides her true identity and serves her new mistress well until she and Radamés, a captain in the Egyptian army, fall in love. Amneris also loves the captain and her jealousy leads her to betray him. Radamés is sentenced to death as a traitor and Aida must choose between loyalty to her country or death with her true love. *(Harcourt Brace, 1990. 32 pp. Reading Level: 4.0)*

About the Author

For many years Leontyne Price was a star of the Metropolitan Opera. Her first grand performance of *Aida* was given in San Francisco in 1957. She has won nineteen Grammy Awards, three Emmy Awards, the National Medal of Arts and the Presidential Medal of Freedom. She says that Aida is a portrait of her inner self and that while performing the role she was expressing herself "as an American, as a woman and as a human being." Ms. Price feels that we should all aspire to the qualities that Aida represents—love of country, strength and courage.

About the Illustrators

Leo and Diane Dillon were awarded the Caldecott Medal in two consecutive years. They graduated from the Parsons School of Design and for many years were on the faculty of the School of Visual Arts. They live in Brooklyn, New York, with their artist son, Lee.

Before Reading Activity

Who Am I? Game

Introduce children to ancient Egypt with this fun guessing game. First, make a set of eight cards containing words that have to do with ancient Egypt. Give out the eight cards (one at a time) to eight different children. The child with the card answers questions from the group with yes or no. If the word is not guessed by the time five questions are asked, the student can show the card.

sample cards

After Reading Activities

Questions to Think About

After reading *Aida*, ask the children to think about the following questions and share their answers.

1. What were the consequences when Aida broke the rules and went beyond the boundaries?

2. Why do you think Aida kept secret the fact that she was a princess?

3. Suppose a warrior other than Radamés had been chosen to lead the army. How would the story change?

4. What role did jealousy play in the story?

5. If you were Aida would you have left Radamés and returned to your own country? Why or why not?

6. List all the words you can to describe Aida. Which one word in your list best describes her? Why?

About the Pyramids

Using the handout on page 14, have the children do this simple report writing exercise.

Internet Activities

A worksheet containing Internet activities on ancient Egypt and *Aida* can be found on page 15.
Answers for Egypt Activity: 1. T; 2. T; 3. T; 4. T; 5. F; 6. T; 7. F; 8. T

Answers for Opera Activity: Verdi did reimburse the man for his expenses but had the man sign a letter that he would never again attend a Verdi opera.

Additional Reading

More About Opera and the Land of Egypt

Husain, Shahrukh. *Barefoot Book of Stories from the Opera*. MacMillan, 1997. 80 pp. RL: 4.0. A colorful book with stories from seven operas including *The Flying Dutchman, Hansel and Gretel* and *The Magic Flute*.

Parker, Lewis K. *Egypt*. Rourke, 1994. 64 pp. RL: 3.0. Easy-to-understand text with maps describing the people of Egypt and how they live.

Climo, Shirley. *Egyptian Cinderella*. HarperCollins, 1989. 32 pp. RL: 3.0. Like Aida, Rodophes is captured and brought to Egypt as a slave but finally finds happiness as the Pharaoh's bride.

Adinolfi, JoAnn. The *Egyptian Polar Bear*. Houghton Mifflin, 1994. 32 pp. RL: 2.0. A polar bear who has traveled to Egypt befriends the boy king.

Rosenberg, Jane. *Sing Me a Story: The Metropolitan Opera's Book of Opera Stories for Children*. Thomas and Hudson, 1996. 124 pp. RL: 6.0. A retelling of fifteen opera stories, including *Aida*, with twenty-nine full color illustrations.

About the Pyramids

In *Aida*, Radamés was buried in an underground vault. The Pharaohs, however, were buried in elaborate tombs with many rooms called pyramids. Buried along with the Pharaoh were all his earthly possessions that he might need in the afterlife. One of the most famous of these pyramids was that of the Pharaoh Cheops. Read about it in the Data Bank and use the information in the pattern that follows.

A Pyramid Data Bank (The Great Pyramid)

Location	**Description**	**Contents**
Egypt	754ft X 754ft	Tomb for Pharaoh
West bank of Nile	2,300,000 stone blocks	Pharaoh's treasures
In the desert	16 million cubic feet	Religious writings
	Hidden passages & trapdoors	Servants and pets

Uses	**Other Facts**
Stone computer	Took 80,000 men five years to build the Great Pyramid
Observatory	Most tombs robbed of treasures within 200 years of
Burial place	completion
Giant calendar	Mummies sometimes buried with model dolls
Sundial	Went out of fashion between 1800 BC and 800BC
	96 pyramids in Egypt
	King Cheops's body missing from the Great Pyramid

Report using this pattern:

1. The most unusual thing about the Great Pyramid is _____.
   List four to six additional facts.

   _____

   _____

   _____

   But the most unusual thing about the Great Pyramid is _____.

2. Use this same pattern to report on a character from *Aida*.
   Begin your report with the words:
   The most memorable thing about _____ is _____.

   _____

   _____

   _____

   But the most memorable thing about _____ is_____.

From *Celebrating the Coretta Scott King Awards*. Copyright © 2000 by Nancy Polette. (Alleyside Press, 2000)

Internet Activities

Activity 1: Ancient Egypt

Guess yes or no to the following questions. Support or deny your guesses by visiting this website:

> **Mr. Dowling's Electronic Passport—Ancient Egypt**
> http://www.mrdowling.com/604egypt.html

1. _____ Civilizations of ancient Egypt were built along the Amazon River.

2. _____ Most of Egypt is dry desert.

3. _____ Paper was a great invention in ancient Egypt.

4. _____ A mummy is a Pharaoh wrapped in linen when he or she died.

5. _____ Egyptians used leaves from trees to make paper.

6. _____ A scribe is a person who kept records and wrote letters.

7. _____ An oasis is dry desert land.

8. _____ The pyramids were very difficult to build.

Activity 2: About the Opera, *Aida*

Giuseppe Verdi wrote the music for the opera and when a man named Prospero Bertani went to listen to *Aida* at Reggio Emilia, Italy, he was not satisfied with it. He wrote Verdi asking to be reimbursed for expenses. Do you think Verdi should pay the man who did not like his opera? Give reasons he should and should not.

Should	Should Not

Find out what Verdi did at this website:

> **Opera Web—Curious Things**
> http://www.opera.it/English/Opere/Aida/Curiosit.html

3
Beat the Story-Drum, Pum-Pum

Written and Illustrated by Ashley Bryan
1980 Illustrator Award Winner

About the Book

Here are five Nigerian folktales retold in language as rhythmic as the beat of a story-drum. In "Hen and Frog," Frog learns the hard way that being helpful can have its rewards and that laziness can result in disaster. "Why the Bush Cow and Elephant Are Bad Friends" tells of two animals that are so big and so proud that neither will give way to the other when they meet. Tagwayi was "The Husband Who Counted the Spoonfuls," not because he suspected his wife was not feeding him enough, but simply because he liked to count. No wife, however, would put up with this rude habit. In yet another tale the author tells "Why Frog and Snake Never Play Together." The two were, in fact, good playmates until their parents objected and warned their off-spring never again to go near each other.

The final story in the collection tells "How Animals Got Their Tails." It seems that when the Great Spirit created flies, the other animals were most unhappy because the flies were biting every animal in sight. Since flies could not be eliminated, the Great Spirit agreed to give animals tails to swish them away. This worked well except for rabbit who ended up with a very short tail since he refused to go and get his new tail himself. *(Coward McCann, 1979. 32 pp. Reading Level: 2.0)*

About the Author/Illustrator

Ashley Bryan grew up in New York City, one of six children. He says his childhood home was filled not only with children but with lots of birds and music. He attended both Columbia University and the Cooper Union Art School and taught art at Dartmouth College. He is a well-known speaker and storyteller as well as an artist and author. His books bring tales alive with a perfect blend of art and text. Other books by Ashley Bryan include *All Night, All Day; The Cat's Purr; Sing to the Sun; The Dancing Granny; Ashley Bryan's ABCs of American Poetry* and many more.

Before Reading Activity

Describe an African Animal

Using the handout on page 18, have the children research their favorite African animal.

After Reading Activities

Questions to Think About

After reading *Beat the Story-Drum, Pum-Pum*, ask the children to think about the following questions and share their answers.

1. How did frog pay for his laziness?

2. Why did hen help frog?

3. What could Bush Cow and Elephant do to get along?

4. Why did the people want Bush Cow and Elephant to like each other?

5. Why were the wives upset at their counting husband?

6. Was counting spoonfuls rude? Why or why not?

7. What happened to end the friendship of frog and snake?

8. Were the parents right not to let them play together? Why or why not?

9. Why did the Creator refuse to get rid of the flies?

10. What lesson does this story teach?

Writing Exercise

Have the children complete this pattern about one of the animals in this book.

I am _____

See me _____

Hear me _____

Touch me and feel_____

Watch me_____

But watch out! I may be watching you.

Mystery Animal Game

Choose an animal from this story to read about. List four clues about the animal. One must be a "give away" clue. Ask a member of the group to give you a number between one and four. Read the clue for that number. The student can guess or pass. The game continues until the animal name is guessed or all clues have been read.

<u>Examples</u>

1. I have legs fourteen inches around.

2. I mostly sleep during the day.

3. I am the King of the Beasts ("*give away*" *clue*)

4. I eat meat. (*Answer: lion*)

Internet Activity

Using the worksheet on page 19, plan a special Elephant Day and have the children do a variety of activities about elephants.

Paper Bag Puppets

Hand out the directions on page 20 and let the children create paper bag puppets. Have them use their puppets to retell a scene from one of the stories.

Additional Reading

More African Folktales

Olaleye, Isaac. *Bitter Bananas*. Boyds Mill. 1994. 32 pp. RL: 2.0. An African boy outwits the baboons who are stealing the palm sap.

Kurtz, Jane. *Fire on the Mountain*. Simon & Schuster, 1994. 32 pp. RL: 2.0. An African legend about a young shepherd who outwits his rich master.

Lottridge, Celia Barker. *Name of the Tree*. Macmillan, 1989. 32 pp. RL: 3.0. A folktale about African animals searching for food during a drought.

Shelf Medearis, Angela. *Singing Man: Adapted from a West AFrican Folktale*. Holiday House, 1994. 32 pp. RL: 2.0. A Nigerian folktale about a boy who leaves home and family to become a musician.

Gerson, Mary Joan. *Why the Sky is Far Away: A Nigerian Folktale*. Little, Brown, 1992. 32 pp. RL: 2.0. An African folktale that tells why people today must grow and harvest their own food.

Describe an African Animal

Research your favorite African animal from *Beat the Story-Drum, Pum-Pum*. Answer the following questions and share the information with the class. A sample is provided below.

Name: African Lion
How tall/long? 5 to 8 feet
How heavy? 350-550 lbs.
What does it eat? Giraffes, warthogs and baby elephants
What does it do for fun? Climbs trees and leaps over deep ditches
How does it usually feel? Quiet and peaceful until its stomach growls
What do you think is most important about the lion? It's called the King of the beasts.

Name: _____

How tall/long? _____

How heavy? _____

What does it eat? _____

What does it do for fun? _____

How does it usually feel? _____

What do you think is most important about the _____?

_____

Internet Activity

One of the stories in *Beat the Story-Drum, Pum-Pum* tells why Bush Cow and Elephant are Bad Friends. But, elephants can also be our very good friends. Visit this Internet site for lots of ideas on celebrating an Elephant Day.

> **WildHeart Productions—Elephant Appreciation Day**
> http://wildheart.com/eday/main_eday.html

Try some of these activities at the site:

Find out what an elephant breakfast is.

Learn an elephant dance.

Read and elephant poem.

Work an elephant puzzle.

Take an elephant quiz.

Color elephant pages.

You can also design your own Elephant Day Flag. Draw a sketch of your flag below.

From *Celebrating the Coretta Scott King Awards*. Copyright © 2000 by Nancy Polette. (Alleyside Press, 2000)

Paper Bag Puppets

Follow the directions and create a paper bag animal puppet. Use your puppet to retell a scene from one of the stories in *Beat the Story-Drum, Pum-Pum.*

What You Need

One small paper lunch bag, paper for drawing, scissors, glue, crayons, colored pencils or markers

What to Do

1. Color a head with crayons, colored pencils or markers and then cut out.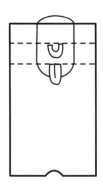

2. Glue head to the bottom of folded small paper lunch bag.

3. With bottom of bag folded back, draw the inside of the mouth and a tongue.

4. Color the inside of the mouth black and the tongue and throat opening red.

5. To make your bag puppet talk, put your thumb against your hand in the bag and move your hand like you are waving.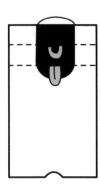

6. Use your puppet to retell a scene from one of the stories.

Christmas in the Big House, Christmas in the Quarters

Written & Illustrated by Patricia & Frederick McKissack
1995 Author Award Winner

About the Book

It is Christmastime on a plantation in Virginia. The year is 1859. The Big House is awash with light, color, elegance and beauty at every turn. There is delicious food and warm hospitality. But along with the carols and the gifts, there is talk of John Brown's raid, the slave uprisings, secession and war. In the slave quarters nearby, there is no such grandeur for the families who live in cramped quarters with dirt floors. Yet despite the harshness of their lives, today a joyous celebration is going on with eating, singing and dancing. Some slaves who were sold away are reunited with those they love, if only for a day. Their songs and stories are filled with hope that somehow they will be free one day. *(Scholastic, 1994. 68 pp. Reading Level: 5.0)*

About the Authors/Illustrators

Patricia and Fredrick McKissack are three-time Coretta Scott King Award winners for both fiction and nonfiction. Patricia grew up in Nashville, Tennessee, where she lived with caring grandparents who gave her a love of books and reading. She remembers many nights reading aloud to her grandfather and hearing her grandmother's stories. Her love of literature led her to a teaching profession and from there to editing children's books

for Concordia Publishing Company. Patricia and Fred have their own company, All Writing Services, and often team in the writing of children's books, both fiction and nonfiction.

Before Reading Activities

Christmas on the Plantation

Have the children think about things the children in the Big House and the children in the Quarters might see at Christmastime. A handout for this activity appears on page 23.

Answers to Activity: Sites in the Big House would be a lace tablecloth, stockings, Yule Log, stone fireplace, toys, harp, Hunter's Brunch, apples and roast turkey. Sites in the Quarters would be gourds, stockings, cornbread, apples, pallets, water-soaked stump, pinecones and possum.

After Reading Activities

Questions to Think About

After reading *Christmas in the Big House, Christmas in the Quarters*, ask the children to think about the following questions and share their answers.

1. Suppose that the folks from the Big House and the slaves celebrated each other's Christmas for one day. Would either feel differently about the other's life? How?

2. Some slaves chose not to take part in joining the family on the porch on Christmas Eve night even though they might be out of favor later. Why do you think they did this?

3. What would the slave children find in their stockings? How would their gifts be different from the gifts received by the children in the Big House?

4. What was the biggest worry of the people in the Big House? What was the biggest worry of the slaves?

5. What were pit schools? Why were they important?

6. What one thing do you think any slave child would want for Christmas more than anything else? Why?

A Christmas Stocking

Using the stocking pattern on page 24, have the children draw gifts it might contain if hung in the Quarters.

What Have You Learned About the Life of a Slave?

Hand out copies of the worksheet on page 25 and have the children answer "yes" or "no" to the questions about slavery. A simple writing assignment about famous abolitionists is also on this sheet.
Answers to Activity 1: Questions 1–10 are all yes.

Internet Activity on the Underground Railroad

Using the worksheet on page 26, have the children answer the questions on the Underground Railroad, then go to the Internet site provided to check their answers.

Answers to the Activity: 1. an escape route for slaves; 2. a passenger on the railroad; 3. safe house; 4. slaves; 5. no; 6. 2,500; 7. walk across the ice or take a boat; 8. yes

Additional Reading

More About Christmas & Kwanzaa

Rylant, Cynthia. *Children of Christmas.* Franklin Watts, 1993. 64 pp. RL: 4.0. Six short stories about diverse ways in which Christmas is celebrated.

Greenfield, Eloise and Lessie Jones Little. Illus. by Jerry Pinkney. *Childtimes: A Three Generation Memoir.* HarperCollins, 1993. 64 pp. RL: 4.0. A lyrical memoir in which three generations of African women recall their childhoods.

Rollins, Charlemae, ed. Illus. by Ashley Bryan. *Christmas Gif': An Anthology of Christmas Poems, Songs and Stories Written By and About African-Americans.* Morrow, 1993. 32 pp. RL: 2.0. A collection of Christmas prose and poetry featuring African American themes and characters.

Silverman, Jerry, ed. *Christmas Songs.* Chelsea House, 1992. 64 pp. RL: 5.0. A collection of popular African American songs on Christmas themes with historical notes.

Burden-Patmon, Denise. *Imani's Gift at Kwanzaa.* Simon & Schuster, 1993. 48 pp. RL: 3.0. A young child celebrates this African American holiday.

Christmas on the Plantation

It is Christmastime on the plantation. Put the letter B before sights that a child in the Big House might see. Put the letter "Q" before a sight the child in the slave quarters might see. Put both letters on the line if the sight is one both children would see. Guess if you do not know.

After hearing or reading *Christmas in the Big House, Christmas in the Quarters,* see how many of your guesses were right.

_____ lace tablecloth   _____ Yule log

_____ water-soaked stump   _____ stone fireplace

_____ miniature toys   _____ pinecones

_____ gourds   _____ cinnamon apples

_____ Hunter's Brunch   _____ stockings

_____ pallets   _____ roast turkey

_____ shortcakes   _____ harp

_____ possum

A Christmas Stocking

Draw on the outside of this stocking the gifts it might contain if it hung in the Quarters.

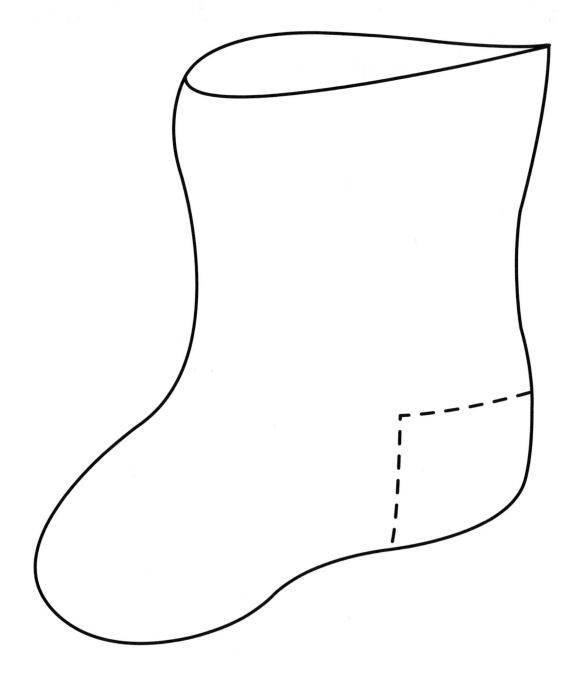

What Have You Learned About the Life of a Slave?

Activity 1

After reading *Christmas in the Big House, Christmas in the Quarters*, mark each statement below yes or no.

1. Many slaves had first names but no last names. _____

2. A corn shuck mattress served as a bed. _____

3. Slave children could be taken from their mothers and sold. _____

4. Slaves were forbidden to learn to read. _____

5. Slaves often did not have enough to eat. _____

7. Some slaves got holiday passes to visit their loved ones. _____

8. Holiday visitors who brought their personal slaves had them sleep on the floor in the hall. _____

9. A slave caught reading the *North Star* newspaper would be in trouble. _____

10. Pit schools were set up to teach slave children to read and write. _____

Activity 2

William Lloyd Garrison, Susan B. Anthony, Harriet Tubman and Frederick Douglass helped the slaves in many ways. Read about two of these abolitionists and use information about them in the pattern below.

If I were _____ I would _____

and _____

and I'd _____

but I wouldn't _____

because _____ did that.

The Underground Railroad on the Internet

At the end of *Christmas in the Big House, Christmas in the Quarters,* a slave mother holds her son who tells her that within the next year he is going to run away to freedom.

One escape route for fugitive slaves was the Underground Railroad. Work with a partner to answer these questions. Guess if you do not know the answer, then take a virtual ride on the Underground Railroad to support or deny your guesses.

1. What was the Underground Railroad?

2. What was it that Harriet Tubman never lost?

3. What did a lantern on a hitching post mean?

4. Who traveled on the railroad?

5. Were the slaves safe when they reached a free state?

6. How many miles through the Appalachian Mountains did the slaves have to travel to reach Rochester, New York?

7. What were the two ways slaves could cross Lake Erie into Canada and freedom?

8. Could former slaves vote and own land in Canada?

Find the answers by riding the Underground Railroad at this website:

National Geographic—The Underground Railroad http://www.nationalgeographic.com/features/99/railroad/j1a.html

Cornrows

Illustrated by Carole Byard, Written by Camille Yarbrough
1980 Illustrator Award Winner

About the Book

Sister and her brother "Metoo" watch their Great-Grammaw braid their mother's hair in cornrows. As she watches, Sister learns the meaning of the many cornrow hair styles. Mother's style is called suku which in Yoruba means basket. Then Great-Grammaw begins to tell the children of the many African symbols for courage, honor, wisdom, love and strength. The braided hair could symbolize the village a woman came from. The number of braids denoted a princess, a queen or a bride, and the pattern of the braids would tell about the gods they worshiped. Then Great-Grammaw's story changes and she tells of the slavers who came and put the people in chains to be sold to the highest bidder. But the spirit behind the symbols did not die and lives on in the accomplishments of many African Americans: Paul Robeson, Malcolm X, Martin Luther King, Jr., Rosa Parks, Katherine Dunham, Aretha Franklin, Langston Hughes and many more. (*Coward McCann, 1979. 48 pp. Reading Level: 3.5*)

About the Author

Camille Yarbrough has been an actress, composer and singer and has appeared often on television and in the theater. She was a member of both the New York and touring companies of *To Be Young, Gifted and Black*. She has recorded her songs and dialogues and has received a Fellowship Grant from the National Endowment for the Arts. In addition to *Cornrows*, her other books for children include *Little Tree Growin' in the Shade, Shimmershine Queens,* and *Tamika and the Wisdom Rings*. She was born and raised in Chicago.

About the Illustrator

Carole Byard was born in Atlantic City, New Jersey. She studied at the Fleischer Art memorial in Philadelphia and at the New York Phoenix School of Design. Her paintings have appeared in many exhibitions. She has illustrated many books for children including *Africa Dream* by Eloise Greenfield and *Three African Tales* by Adjai Robinson.

Before Reading Activitiy

Topic Talking

Assign partners within the group. State a topic, such as freedom, and have partner A talk on the topic. After 10 seconds, say "Switch." Have partner B talk on the same subject for 10 seconds until you say "Stop."

Follow this procedure with a second topic, increasing the time to 15 seconds, and a third topic for 20 seconds. Over a period of time, slowly increase the amount of time *and* the size of the group.

Guidelines for Topic Talking

1. Topics should be those that students know something about.

2. Topics can be assigned and time allowed for preparation.

3. As students become comfortable with Topic

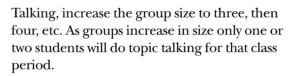

Talking, increase the group size to three, then four, etc. As groups increase in size only one or two students will do topic talking for that class period.

4. As a variation of the procedure above, try this: Student A speaks to Student B on a topic for the allotted time. When you say "Switch," Student B tells Student A what he or she said until you say "Stop."

5. This activity can be used at any grade level.

After Reading Activities

Questions to Think About

After reading *Cornrows*, ask the children to think about the following questions and share their answers.

1. What is a symbol? Why are symbols important?

2. Do you think an African queen still wore her hair in cornrows after she was made a slave? Why or why not?

3. How did the slaves keep alive the spirit of love, courage, honor, wisdom and strength?

4. Why was giving a name to her cornrows so important to Sister?

A Food Chant

Hand out the worksheet on page 29 and have the children write a chant about their favorite food in the pattern of the sample provided.

An Internet Research Activity

Have the children pick a famous person from *Cornrows* and read about that person's life on the Internet. Then have them write a report in the style of the sample provided on page 30.

Additional Reading

Lives of Famous African Americans

Marzollo, Jean. *Happy Birthday Martin Luther King.* Random House, 1985. 32 pp. RL: 2.0. A simple and moving introduction to the civil rights leader's life and to the holiday that honors him.

Livingston, Myra Cohn. *Keep on Singing: A Ballad of Marian Anderson.* Holiday House, 1994. 32 pp. RL: 2.0. A biography in rhyming test about the African American singer.

Livingston, Myra Cohn. *Let Freedom Ring: A Ballad of Martin Luther King, Jr.* Holiday House, 1992. 32 pp. RL: 2.0. A retelling in ballad form of the life and words of Martin Luther King, Jr.

Keenan, Sheila. *Frederick Douglass: Portrait of a Freedom Fighter.* Scholastic, 1995. 32 pp. RL: 2.0. A picture book biography of Douglass's life from birth as a slave to becoming a free man.

A Food Chant

Read the following corn chant. Use the same pattern to write a chant about another food.

Corn Chant

We like corn

   Tall corn

   Green corn

   Yellow corn

   Sweet corn

   Ripe corn

   Growing growing

These are just a few

   Corn fritters

   Corn cakes

   Cornbread

   Corn relish

   Creamed corn

   Buttered corn

   Popcorn, too

   Healthy food

   Happy mood

We like corn

We like _____

_____ _____

_____ _____

_____ _____

_____ _____

_____ _____

_____ _____

_____ _____

These are just a few

_____ _____

_____ _____

_____ _____

_____ _____

_____ _____

_____ _____

_____,too

Healthy food

Happy mood

We like _____

Internet Research Activity

Choose one of the famous people mentioned in this book. Read about his or her life on the Internet and write a Fortunately/Unfortunately report about the person. Follow the example given below which tells the both the good and not so good things that happened in the life of George Washington Carver.

Sample Fortunately/Unfortunately Report for George Washington Carver

Fortunately George Washington Carver revolutionized the agriculture of the South.

Unfortunately he was born of slave parents and lost his mother to a band of night raiders.

Fortunately he was able to attend Simpson College.

Unfortunately he had to earn his way by cooking, taking in laundry and working as a janitor.

Fortunately he received an appointment at Iowa State University as an assistant botanist.

Unfortunately he made very little money during his lifetime.

Fortunately he discovered over 300 uses for the peanut and received the Roosevelt Medal for his many contributions to science.

You can use one of the websites below to find information for your fortunately/unfortunately report:

Katherine Dunham
http://www.kennedy-center.org/honors/years/dunham.html
Aretha Franklin
http://wallofsound.go.com/artists/arethafranklin/home.html
Langston Hughes
http://mickey.queens.lib.ny.us/special/langston.bio.html
Richard Wright
http://gwis2.circ.gwu.edu/~cuff/wright/
Paul Robeson
http://www.cs.uchicago.edu/cpsr/robeson/bio.html

From *Celebrating the Coretta Scott King Awards*. Copyright © 2000 by Nancy Polette. (Alleyside Press, 2000)

The Creation

Illustrated by James E. Ransome, Written by James Weldon Johnson
1995 Illustrator Award Winner

About the Book

The Creation was written in 1919 to be included in a book titled *God's Trombones: Seven Negro Sermons in Verse*. It tells the story of God's creation of the world beginning with the sun, the moon and the stars. Next came the Earth and the oceans; then the grass and the flowers, the beasts and the birds. But as God looked at his creation he was lonely, so he scooped up a lump of clay from the river and shaped a man in his own image. Then he blew the breath of life into man and his creation was complete. *(Holiday House, 1994. 32 pp. Reading Level: 3.0)*

About the Author

James Weldon Johnson was an amazing man for his time. He was born in 1871 shortly after the close of the Civil War. He attended Atlanta and Columbia Universities and was admitted to the Florida bar in 1897. He was a man of many talents. He worked as a high school principal, wrote the libretto for an opera performed at the Metropolitan Opera House in 1915, and served as United Stated Consul in Nicaragua and Venezuela. He was also an artist and an adept administrator, serving as secretary of the National Association for the Advancement of Colored People. He died in an automobile accident in 1938.

About the Illustrator

James E. Ransome was born in North Carolina but lived in New Jersey as a teenager. He studied art at the Pratt Institute and in addition to illustrating The Creation, he also is praised for his illustrations in *Celie and the Harvest Fiddler* by Vanessa and Valerie Flournoy, *My Best Shoes* by Denise Lewis Patrick, *How Many Stars in the Sky?* by Lenny Hort and *The Wagon* by Tony Johnston who was inspired to write the text after viewing the artist's painting, *Carolina Morning*. Mr. Ransome lives in Poughkeepsie, New York, with his wife, Lesa, and their two daughters.

Before Reading Activity

Story String

Make a set of cards for each of the children containing the following words: *sun, moon, stars, mountain, tree, flower, fish* and *rabbit*. Punch a hole in the top and bottom of each card. Let the children string the cards on yarn in the order in which they think the items will be created in the story. After hearing the story the order can be changed.

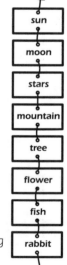

sample string

After Reading Activities

Questions to Think About

After reading *The Creation*, ask the children to think about the following questions and share their answers.

1. In the poem how did God make the seven seas?

2. How did he make the thunder and lightning?

3. How did he make the rain fall?

4. Suppose God had created the fish before he created the seas. What would have happened?

5. Suppose God created the animals before he created the trees and other plants. What problems would the animals have?

6. Is doing a job in the correct order sometimes very important? Why or why not?

Song and Writing Activity

Using the handout on page 33, have the children sing "A Changing Song," then have them write their own song.

Create the Changing Seasons

For this craft, you will need the following items for each child: thin white paper 6"x18"; water color paints; five pieces of sponge about 1" square; five clip clothespins; and a paintbrush.

<u>What to Do</u>

1. Fold your paper in half and then in half again. Wet paper under the faucet.

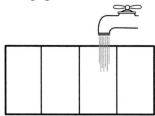

3. While the paper is wet, paint blue strips and let the paint bleed down. This makes the sky.

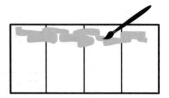

4. When the paper dries, paint a brown tree on each part.

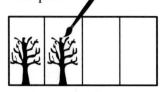

5. Make the first tree look like summer, the second tree look like fall, the third tree like winter ad the last tree like spring. Use the sponges clipped to clothespins to dab on the paint.

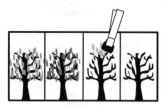

Internet Activity

Using the handout on page 34, have the children do the activity on habitats.

<u>Answers to Habitat Activity</u>: *Grasslands: gray wolf, beetle, bison, kit fox, puma, coyote, bobcat. Oceans: mollusk, whale, dolphin, eel, shark. Deserts: gila monster, scorpion, lizard, kangaroo rat. Mountains: llama, snow leopard, eagle, falcon.*

Additional Reading

African Creation Stories

Roth, Susan L. *Fire Came to the Earth People.* Dial, 1994. 32 pp. RL: 2.0. A creation myth from Africa based on a Dahomean myth.

Gerson, Mary-Joan. *How Night Came From the Sea.* Little, Brown, 1994. 32 pp. RL: 3.0. A story of how an African sea goddess brought night to the land of daylight.

Aardema, Verna. *How the Ostrich Got Its Long Neck.* Scholastic, 1995. 32 pp. RL: 2.5. A humorous African Folktale that explains how the ostrich got its unusual shape.

Anderson, David A. *Origin of Life on Earth: An African Creation Myth.* Sights, 1991. 32 pp. RL: 2.0. A visual retelling of a Yoruba legend of how the world began.

A Changing Song

Many changes took place in *The Creation*. First came the sun, moon and stars. Then the mountains, oceans and rivers were formed. Fish were added to the waters, and trees and flowers grew from the land. Finally animals and man were created.

Let's sing this song about the changes in an apple tree. Sing the song to the tune of "I'm A Little Teapot."

Changes

Look at the apple tree
That grew from a seed
Slowly, slowly from a seed
In the soil it grew and grew
Look at the apple tree
It's looking at you.

Use the song pattern to write about something else that changes. You can write about a violet growing from a seed, a gull hatching from an egg or anything else that changes

Look at the _____

That grew from a _____

Slowly, slowly from a _____

In the _____

It grew and grew

Look at the _____

It's brand new.

Internet Activity

Activity: Habitats

A habitat is a place where a particular animal or species lives. Examples of habitats are deserts, oceans, grasslands and mountains. A habitat suitable for one animal is not necessarily suitable for another.

In *The Creation,* many animals are placed on the Earth. Each animal needs to be placed in its proper habitat.

Visit the following Habitats & Biomes website to see where these animals live. Then place each one in its proper habitat by writing the habitat number on the line before the animal name.

Habitats & Biomes
http://library.thinkquest.org/11922/habitats/habitats.htm

Habitats: 1. Grasslands; 2. Oceans ; 3. Deserts; 4. Mountains

_____ llama		_____ whale	
_____ scorpion		_____ coyote	
_____ gray wolf		_____ gila monster	
_____ puma		_____ eagle	
_____ beetle		_____ kit fox	
_____ eel		_____ lizard	
_____ bison		_____ snow leopard	
_____ shark		_____ falcon	
_____ mollusk		_____ dolphin	
_____ kangaroo rat		_____ bobcat	

7

The Dark Thirty
Southern Tales of the Supernatural

Written by Patricia McKissack, Illustrated by Brian Pinkney
1993 Author Award Winner

About the Book

The dark thirty refers to that thirty minutes just before nightfall, that time in the deepening twilight when things are not clearly seen. It is a time for families to gather and to listen to their elders relate the scary tales passed down to them from earlier generations. Some of the tales might be about real people in scary situations like the little girl who has to confront the monster in the chicken house. Others might have been sourced in fact but grew in the telling like "The Legend of Pin Oak" where slaves would rather leap from a high cliff to their deaths than be captured. Still other tales grew from professions like "The 11:59" told by the Pullman car porters. Regardless of the source, here is a collection of ten hair-raising tales rooted in African American history and the oral storytelling tradition. Each is memorable and each lets the reader experience the delicious horror of a tale of the dark thirty. *(Knopf, 1992. 122 pp. Reading Level: 6.0)*

About the Author

Patricia C. McKissack grew up in Tennessee, attended Tennessee State University and Webster University in St. Louis, Missouri. She taught eighth grade while her twin sons were growing up and became editor of children's books at Concordia Publishing. Pat and her husband, Fred, decided to become a full-time writing team and started their own company, All-Writing Services. Working together, their titles range from a definitive work on the civil rights movement in America, to the pre-school Messy Bessy series to the award-winning picture book, *Mirandy and Brother Wind.*

About the Illustrator

Brian Pinkney, the son of an artist father, was born and raised in New York where he lives today. His original scratchboard illustrations have won many awards including a Caldecott.

Before Reading Activities

Find Someone Who...

Copy the worksheet on page 37 and give to each child. Have the children "interview" others in the group to find out who has something in common with the characters in *The Dark Thirty.*

Brainstorming

Have a brainstorming session with your group using the following topics:

1. Name ways a person could jump off a high cliff and escape injury.

2. Name ways a slave might defy his owner with no consequences.

3. How many stories can you cite that have revenge as a theme?

4. Brainstorm all the tasks a Pullman porter was expected to do.

5. List all the ways that the ability to tell the future might be a curse.

6. What are the many problems a snowstorm can bring?

7. What are all the advantages of having a brother?

8. Give as many reasons as you can that the creature Bigfoot cannot exist.

9. Name as many household dangers as you can.

After Reading Activities

Discussing the Stories

Give small groups one question related to the story. The group discusses the question for five minutes. At the end of discussion time, ideas are shared with the class.

1. "The Legend of Pin Oak." Did Henri, Charlemae and their child escape or did they die and undergo transformation into beautiful birds? Explain your answer.

2. "We Organized." Suppose the slaves had not had a "massa's" button to pin on the straw doll. Would the results have been the same? Why or why not?

3. "Justice." Why do you think Hoop saw cloudy windows when no one else did?

4. "The 11:59." Suppose Lester had not worked for the railroad. What other significant time might have been related to his death? Why?

5. "The Sight." Was Esau better off with or without the sight? Why?

6. "The Woman in the Snow." List as many ways as you can that this story and the fairy tale "Rapunzel" are alike.

7. "The Conjure Brother." Did Madame Zinnia actually exist or did Josie make up a friend to help her with her troubles? Explain.

8. "Boo Mama." Do you think this story might actually have happened? Why or why not?

9. "The Gingi." What is superstition? What examples of superstition can you name? What examples of superstition are found in this story?

10. "The Chicken-Coop Monster." How is this story related to the famous saying of President Franklin D. Roosevelt when he told people at the beginning of World War II, "The only thing we have to fear is fear itself."

Melissa's Chicken Coop Monster

Hand out the patterns on page 38 and have the children make their own Chicken Coop Monster.

Writing About Feelings

Have the group think about the many different feelings the characters experienced in *The Dark Thirty*. Then do the writing assignment on page 39.

Internet Activities

Two Internet activities, one on slavery and one on Sasquatch sightings, can be found on the handout on page 40.

Answers to Slavery Activity: 1. yes; 2. no; 3. no; 4. yes; 5. yes; 6. yes; 7. no; 8 yes; 9. yes. Key word: INJUSTICE

Additional Reading

More Spine Tingling Tales

Marin, Jr., Bill, and John Archambault. *Ghost-Eye Tree*. Harcourt Brace, 1985. 32 pp. RL: 2.0. A brother and sister walking together late at night argue over who is afraid of the ghost-eye tree.

Giovanni, Nikki. *Genie in the Jar*. Holt, 1996. 32 pp. RL: 2.0. A lyrical song of freedom but also warns of the pain it can bring.

Haskins, Jim. *The Headless Haunt and Other African-American Ghost Stories*. HarperCollins, 1994. 112 pp. RL: 4.0. Ghost tales from African folklore and personal accounts of slaves.

Sierra, Judy. Illus. by Jerry Pinkney. *Wiley and the Hairy Man*. Dutton, 1996. 32 pp. RL: 2.0. Wiley must fool a swamp monster three times to be rid of it.

Find Someone Who...

Find out what members of your class or group have in common with the characters and situations in *The Dark Thirty*. For each item that follows find someone in your group who can claim to have had the experience. Put a different name on each line.

Find Someone Who...

1. Knows what a mansion is.

   _____

2. Has one brother.

   _____

3. Can name a beautiful bird that is larger than a chicken.

   _____

4. Can give the purpose of the Underground Railroad.

   _____

5. Has been falsely accused of a misdeed.

   _____

6. Can explain the difference between revenge and justice.

   _____

7. Has ridden on a train.

   _____

8. Knows what a Sasquatch is.

   _____

Melissa's Chicken Coop Monster

Cut out and combine these parts to create the monster Melissa might have imagined was in the chicken house.

Writing about Feelings

Many of the stories in *The Dark Thirty* deal with prejudice and injustice. The characters felt fear, compassion, love, despair, loneliness, resentment, and anger.

For this writing assignment, you will choose a character from one of the stories in *The Dark Thirty* and an emotion that fits with them. Write about the feeling as if you were the character. Follow the pattern in the example below, which uses Melissa from "The Chicken Coop Monster" as the character and fear as the emotion.

Melissa Speaks
I am fear.
Breathlessness and dark thoughts surround me.
I cannot escape bones chilled with cold.
I live with cowardice and trepidation.
I spend my days making helpers of unsuspecting victims.
My cousins are darkness and terror.
Dressed as I am in the black cloak of night.
The gifts I bestow are rapid heartbeats and cold sweats.
I am fear.

I am (*name the feeling*) _____

I am surrounded by _____

I cannot escape _____

I live with _____

I spend my days _____

My cousins are _____

My clothing is _____

I give to those I touch _____

I am (*repeat the first line*) _____

From *Celebrating the Coretta Scott King Awards.* Copyright © 2000 by Nancy Polette. (Alleyside Press, 2000)

Internet Activities

Activity 1: Slavery

The first two stories in *The Dark Thirty* have to do with slavery. Guess the answers to these statements by circling the letter under yes or no. Support or deny your guesses by visiting this website:

> **Afro-Americ@—Africa to America**
> http://www.afroam.org/history/slavery/africa.html

		Yes	No
1.	Most slaves came from the west coast of Africa	I	L
2.	They came chained three by three.	P	N
3.	The Mandingos were a warlike people.	S	J
4.	Slaves were purchased from brokers at forts.	U	T
5.	Slaves were kept in a prison near the beach.	S	C
6.	Slaves were marked with red hot irons.	T	D
7.	Slave ships traveled a southern route.	G	I
8.	Slaves were packed on 18 inch shelves in the ship.	C	O
9.	A slave's life was a nightmare of drudgery.	E	R

Write the letters for each of your answers on these lines. If your answers are correct you will see an important word related to slavery.

___ ___ ___ ___ ___ ___ ___ ___ ___

Activity 2: Sasquatch

The story, "Boo, Mama" tells of the meeting of a woman with a Sasquatch who had saved her child. At this website you can read about alleged sightings of a real Sasquatch or Bigfoot. On a separate sheet of paper, list the similarities you find regarding the creatures in the story and in the news articles. What conclusions can you draw?

> **The Shadowlands—Bigfoot**
> http://theshadowlands.net/bf.htm

8

The Friendship

Written by Mildred D. Taylor, Illustrated by Max Ginsburg
1988 Author Award Winner

About the Book

When Aunt Callie sends Cassie Logan and her brothers for medicine, the four children head nervously for the Wallace store despite their parents' warnings never to go there. And sure enough, they find themselves bracing for trouble as they witness Mr. Tom Bee, an old black man, calling the white storekeeper by his first name. The year is 1933, the place Mississippi, and any child knows that certain things just aren't done. What follows is shocking and unforgettable, but not at all what the children, the former slave or the storekeeper expect. *(Dial, 1987. 56 pp. Reading Level: 5.0)*

About the Author

Mildred D. Taylor was born in Jackson, Mississippi, and grew up in Toledo, Ohio. After two years with the Peace Corps she enrolled in the School of Journalism at the University of Colorado. There she worked with university officials and students in initiating a Black Studies program. She now lives in Colorado. Among her many popular children's books are *Song of the Trees*; *Roll of Thunder, Hear My Cry*; and *Let the Circle Be Unbroken*.

About the Illustrator

Max Ginsburg received his Bachelor of Fine Arts degree from Syracuse University and his Master of Arts from the City College of New York. In addition to painting, he taught at the School of Visual Arts in New York City where his home is. He has received the Gold Medal Award from the Society of Illustrators and has exhibited his paintings in many one-man shows.

Before Reading Activity

Find Someone Who...

Using the handout on page 43, have the children interview others in the group to find out what they have in common with characters in the story.

After Reading Activities

Questions to Think About

After reading *The Friendship*, ask the children to think about the following questions and share their answers.

1. Why were the children warned not to go into Wallace's store?

2. What parts of the story might be different if it had taken place in the year 2000? Why do you think so?

3. Name one thing on which Mr. Tom Bee placed great value. Tell why you chose it.

4. What does "giving your word" mean?

5. List specific incidents of prejudice in the story, What causes prejudice? What are some things that can be done to combat it?

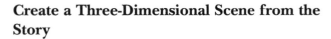

Create a Three-Dimensional Scene from the Story

Directions for this craft appear on page 44.

Assigning Roles in a Folk Musical

Have the children in your group pretend they are the director of a folk musical based on *The Friendship*. A handout for this activity appears on page 45.

Internet Activity

Using the handout on page 46, have the children work alone or in pairs to do this activity on courage.

Additional Reading

More Books by Mildred D. Taylor

Taylor, Mildred D. *Let the Circle Be Unbroken.* Dial, 1981. 395 pp. RL: 7.0. The Logan family enlists the help of the community in an effort to save their farm.

Taylor, Mildred D. *The Road to Memphis.* Dial, 1990. 290 pp. RL: 6.0. Cassie, her brother and his friends face many obstacles and dangers as they travel from Mississippi to Tennessee.

Taylor, Mildred D. *Roll of Thunder, Hear My Cry.* Dial, 1976. 276 pp. RL: 7.0. An African American family struggles during the Depression to hold on to its land.

Taylor, Mildred D. *Song of the Trees.* Dial, 1975. 48 pp. RL: 5.0. Cassie Logan's father manages to save the trees she loves from white loggers.

Find Someone Who...

See what your class or group has in common with the characters and events in *The Friendship*. Find a different name for each line.

Find Someone Who...

1. Can find Mississippi on a map.

   _____

2. Had to wait to be served until all other customers are taken care of.

   _____

3. Calls an adult by his or her first name.

   _____

4. Has done a great favor for a friend.

   _____

5. Has been punished for being disrespectful.

   _____

6. Likes peppermint candy canes.

   _____

7. Likes to go fishing.

   _____

8. Can explain what prejudice is.

   _____

9. Has a nickname.

   _____

10. Has done a favor for a neighbor.

    _____

From *Celebrating the Coretta Scott King Awards*. Copyright © 2000 by Nancy Polette. (Alleyside Press, 2000)

Create a 3-D Scene

Following the directions below, create a three dimensional scene from *The Friendship*.

1. You'll need three sheets of paper—one 8.5"x 10.25" (background), one 8.5"x 9.25" (middleground), and one sheet 8.5"x 8.5" (foreground).

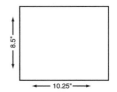

2. In the middle of the background sheet draw a border 6.5"x 7.75", in the middle of the middleground sheet draw a border 6.5"x 6.75", in the middle of the foreground sheet draw a border 5"x 6".

3. Draw and color a background scene on the background sheet. Draw and color in items or characters on the middleground and foreground sheets. (Important: Draw the items on the these sheets next to the border so that when you cut away the area around the items, they will still remain attached to the page.)

4. Cut away the area around the items on the middleground and foreground sheets, taking care to see that they still remain attached to the page.

5. Fold the background and middleground sheets in half to make a vertical crease. Staple or tape the ends of the sheets together flush with each other to complete your 3-D scene.

From *Celebrating the Coretta Scott King Awards.* Copyright © 2000 by Nancy Polette. (Alleyside Press, 2000)

Assigning Roles in a Folk Musical

You are the director of a folk musical based on *The Friendship*. Characters in the musical are Cassie, Stacey, Christopher John, Little Man, Mr. Tom Bee, John Wallace. Which character will you assign to sing the following songs? During which scene from the book will the song be sung?

Song Title: "Just Before the News" **Sung by:** _____

During What Scene? _____

Song Title: "Leave Me Alone" **Sung by:** _____

During What Scene? _____

Song Title: "Angry Eyes" **Sung by:** _____

During What Scene? _____

Song Title: "Walk On By" **Sung by:** _____

During What Scene? _____

Song Title: "My Way" **Sung by:** _____

During What Scene? _____

Song Title: "How Can I Be Sure?" **Sung by:** _____

During What Scene? _____

Song Title: "Fly Like an Eagle" **Sung by:** _____

During What Scene? _____

Song Title: "Long Time" **Sung by:** _____

During What Scene? _____

From *Celebrating the Coretta Scott King Awards*. Copyright © 2000 by Nancy Polette. (Alleyside Press, 2000)

Internet Activity

Activity: Many Faces of Courage

In *The Friendship*, Mr. Tom Bee shows great courage in continuing an act which led to his beating by a group of white men. Here are four African American women who showed great courage. Visit the website for each. Tell in what way each was courageous.

Ida Bell Wells http://library.thinkquest.org/10320/Wells.htm

Showed courage when _____

_____

Mary McLeod Bethune http://greatwomen.org/bethune.htm

Showed courage when _____

_____

Mary Church Terrell http://www.brightmoments.com/blackhistory/nmct.stm

Showed courage when _____

_____

Bessie Coleman http://library.thinkquest.org/10320/Coleman.htm

Showed courage when _____

_____

The websites for Ida Bell Wells and Bessie Coleman show pictures of stamps which were issued in their honor. Design a stamp to honor a great African American living today.

9

Half a Moon and One Whole Star

Illustrated by Jerry Pinkney,
Written by Crescent Dragonwagon
1987 Illustrator Award Winner

About the Book

A young child sleeps, peacefully unaware of the night activity that surrounds her. Under "half a moon and one whole star" robins, parrots and chickens sleep while owls, bats, possums and raccoons awaken to begin their nightly outings. In the city, Johnny gets ready to play his saxophone at the club, bakers are busy at their ovens, while ships at the dock weigh anchor and start their journeys. As night ends, the possums and owls get ready for sleep, Johnny puts away his saxophone, the bakers and the sailors get ready for bed just as Susan awakens for breakfast with her parents. Here is a lullaby of a safe and secure world where children can sleep undisturbed. *(Macmillan, 1986. 32 pp. Reading Level: 2.0)*

About the Author

Crescent Dragonwagon was born and raised in New York City but says she has led a gypsy life. Her mother was children's author and editor, Charlotte Zolotow. Crescent has written more than 40 books including 35 children's books, two novels, a cookbook and a book of poetry. For a time, as a gourmet cook, she ran a restaurant in Eureka Springs, Arkansas. She is a prolific reader which she says helps her to continue to learn as a writer and as a teacher of writing. Among her many popular chil-

dren's books are: *Alligator Arrived with Apples*; *Alligators and Others All Year Long*; *Annie Flies the Birthday Bike*; *Home Place*; *This Is the Bread I Baked for Ned*; and *Winter Holding Spring*.

About the Illustrator

Jerry Pinkney was born in Philadelphia and lives now in Croton-on-Hudson, New York. His books depict the individuality within a black community and his characters are portrayed as naturally as possible. Jerry Pinkney's books have received many awards and his art is shown in many galleries throughout the United States. Jerry's son Brian has followed in his father's footsteps as a children's book illustrator.

Before Reading Activities

Brainstorming

Have the children brainstorm the following topics.

1. Name all the animals you might see if you took a walk in the woods.

2. Name many different workers who work at night.

Animal Riddles

Here are riddles about animals you will meet in this story. Ask: "Who would like to guess the first clue?"

The child called upon can guess or pass. If the answer is not correct or the child passes, ask for a volunteer to try the second clue. The game continues until the animal is guessed or all clues are read. This is an excellent critical listening activity.

Sample Clues

1. I have four legs and fur.
2. My color is gray.
3. I sometimes hang from a tree by my tail.
4. My name rhymes with blossom. (*possum*)

1. My colors are brown and red.
2. I lay eggs.
3. I fold my wings in sleep.
4. My name rhymes with bobbin. (*robin*)

1. I am very small.
2. I have two eyes.
3. I make a noise by rubbing my wings together.
4. My name rhymes with thicket. (*cricket*)

1. I have feathers.
2. I hunt at night.
3. I eat mice.
4. My names rhymes with howl. (*owl*)

After Reading Activities

Responding to the Story

List phrases telling what the animals and people were doing in the woods and in the city.

Example

In the Woods	In the City
robins sleep	bakers count
parrots rest	sailors sail
owls rouse	people talk
possums sniff	Johnny plays
crickets whir	Susan sleeps
raccoons walk	dancers dance

Use two of the items listed in a song sung to the tune of "London Bridges." An example follows.

In the dark woods robins sleep
Robins sleep
Robins sleep
In the dark woods robins sleep
And crickets whir.

Now try using the phrases with "Skip to My Lou."

Robins sleep and parrots rest
Owls rouse and possums sniff
Crickets whir and raccoons walk
In the woods at nighttime.

A Writing Pattern: Where Can You Find?

Have the children use animals or people from the story to complete the writing pattern on page 49.

Internet Activity

Hand out the worksheet on page 50 and have the children do the activitiy about the phases of the moon or send a postcard to a friend.

Additional Reading

More Night Stories

McGuire, Richard. *Night Becomes Day*. Viking, 1994. 32 pp. RL: 2.0. A magical journey from night to day and back again.

Laden, Nina. *The Night I Followed the Dog*. Chronicle Books, 1994. 32 pp. RL: 2.0. A small boy follows his dog on an all night outing.

Rylant, Cynthia. *Night in the Country*. Aladdin, 1986. 32 pp. RL: 2.0. The haunting words and illustrations describe nighttime in the country.

Whitman, Candace. *Night Is Like an Animal*. Farrar, 1985. 32 pp. RL: 1.0. A small child goes to bed and a cozy bear brings on the night.

Greenfield, Eloise. Illus. by Jan Spivey Gilchrist. *Night on Neighborhood Street*. Dial, 1991. 32 pp. RL: 3.0. Seventeen poems describe a childhood surrounded by family, friends and neighbors.

Where Can You Find...?

Use animals or people from the story to complete the pattern.

Example: Where can you find a robin? a parrot? a raccoon? a minnow?
a sleeping child? a saxophone player? a baker? a sailor?

Where can you find a _____?

You could find one _____

And you could see one _____

And one could be _____

But the best place to look is _____

For that is where you will find a _____.

Where can't you find a _____?

It would not be _____

And it would not hide_____

Two places it would never be are_____

Or _____

For that is where you can't find a _____.

Internet Activities

Activity 1: Moon Phases

You can see pictures of the moon in its different phases and find the answers to these questions on this website:

> **StarDate Online—Why does the moon have phases?**
> http://stardate.utexas.edu/resources/faqs/faq.taf?f=answer&id=2

How much of the moon do we see…

1. In the first quarter of its journey around the Earth?

      half   all   none

2. In the second quarter of its journey around the Earth?

      half   all   none

3. In the third quarter of its journey around the Earth?

      half   all   none

4. In the fourth quarter of its journey around the Earth?

      half   all   none

Activity 2: Send a Postcard to a Friend

Visit this website and see four beautiful astronomy postcards. Choose the one you like best and send a message to a friend.

> **Astronomy for Kids—Postcards**
> http://www.dustbunny.com/afk/postcards/postcards.htm

10

Her Stories

African American Folktales, Fairy Tales and True Tales

Written by Virginia Hamilton
Illustrated by Leo & Diane Dillon
1996 Author Award Winner

About the Book

The nineteen stories in this collection focus on the magical lore and wondrous imaginings of African American women. From lighthearted trickster tales to the enchanted world of "Good Blanche, Bad Rose and the Talking Eggs," a broad range of folktales, fairy tales and legendary women are presented. Two of the tales were chosen for activities in this book.

"Catskinella" is a Cinderella tale of a poor girl named Ella whose father wants her to marry a woodsman. She doesn't care for the man and asks help from Mother Mattie, her godmother. Mother Mattie tells the girl to ask her father for a catskin dress and a ring from her husband-to-be. On the wedding day she runs away and finds work in a castle where the prince, seeing her beauty, falls in love with her.

The king commands the maidens of the kingdom to bake the prince a cake. The best cake maker will become his bride. Ella puts the ring in her cake batter and the prince, finding it, is determined to find its owner. When the ring fits only Ella's finger, the prince knows he has found his true love.

In "Good Blanche, Bad Rose, and the Talking Eggs," a mother favors her selfish and ill-mannered daughter, Rose, over sweet-tempered Blanche.

Blanche does all the work while Rose rocks in her chair all day. After being beaten, Blanche runs into the forest where she meets an old woman who takes her in, feeds her and gives her talking eggs. The old woman's strange household shocks Blanche, but she keeps quiet. Following the old woman's directions, Blanche takes only the eggs that say "Take me." The contents turn out to be riches beyond imagining.

When the cruel mother sends Rose to find the old woman, Rose laughs at the woman's house and at the woman herself. She is given the same directions as Blanch regarding the eggs, but she ignores the directions and takes the eggs that say "Don't take me." The contents turn out to be snakes, toads, frogs and whips. The furious mother sees the beasts and whips, and banishes Rose to the woods forever. *(Scholastic, 1995. 112 pp. Reading Level: 5.0)*

About the Author

Virginia Hamilton grew up on a farm in rural Ohio, the youngest of five children. Many of her books reflect her own life: growing up in an extended family, her closeness to her grandparents with their fabulous storehouse of black legend, a love for the small town Midwest, and the lives and relationships of the people who live there. Ms. Hamilton has included among her many awards and honors the following: the 1975 Newbery Medal for *M. C. Higgins, The Great* and a Newbery Honor Book Award and Coretta Scott King Award for *Sweet Whispers, Brother Rush*. Ms. Hamilton lives with her husband, poet Arnold Adoff, in Ohio.

About the Illustrators

Leo and Diane Dillon were awarded the Caldecott Medal in two consecutive years. They graduated from the Parsons School of Design and for many years were on the faculty of the School of Visual Arts. They live in Brooklyn, New York, with their artist son, Lee.

Before Reading Activities

Questions for "Good Blanche, Bad Rose and the Talking Eggs"

Before reading the story, ask the children how they would finish each of the following sentences.

1. Walking alone in the forest is scary but _____ is terrifying!

2. Seeing two arms without bodies, with fists, punching is scary but _____ is terrifying!

3. Watching an old woman take off her head is scary but _____ is terrifying!

4. Scratching a back made of broken glass is scary but _____ is terrifying!

5. Watching a snake pop out of an egg is scary but _____ is terrifying!

"Catskinella" Guessing Game

This game can be played with two to four players. Handout appears on page 54.

Answer to Clues: Bake a cake.

After Reading Activities

Questions to Think About for "Good Blanche, Bad Rose and the Talking Eggs"

After reading "Good Blanche, Bad Rose and the Talking Eggs", ask the children to think about the

following questions and share their answers.

1. Suppose that Blanche's mother had not hit her. How would the story change?

2. Why do you think Blanche rubbed the old woman's back even though she knew it would cut her hand?

3. How may other ways might the old woman have rewarded Blanche without giving her the eggs?

4. Why do you suppose the old woman had Blanche get the eggs herself instead of just giving her the riches?

5. Even though Rose laughed at the old woman, she was given the same instructions as Blanche regarding the eggs. Why did the old woman do this?

6. What lesson is this story teaching?

Questions to Think About for "Catskinella"

1. Compare this story with other Cinderella tales you know. How are they alike and different?

2. Was Ella wrong to run away after she had promised to marry the woodsman? Why or why not?

3. Suppose an ogre had lived in the castle instead of the prince. How might the story change?

4. Was the catskin dress important to the story? Why or why not?

The Story Square

Retell one of the stories using a story square. For each child you will need one large square sheet of white paper and colored pencils.

<u>Directions</u>

1. Fold a square sheet of paper in half and then in half again.

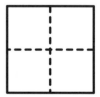

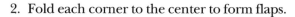

2. Fold each corner to the center to form flaps.

3. Label each flap: character, setting, problem, solution. Put a different heading on each flap.

4. Draw one character under the character flap. Draw one setting under the setting flap. Draw a symbol for the problem under the problem flap. Draw a symbol for the solution under the solution flap.

5. Open all four flaps and draw one item that was most important to the story.

6. On the back of the story square write the title and author of the story.

Making Scratched Talking Eggs

For this activity you will need the following items for each child: manila paper; dark crayons; scissors; unbent paper clip,

<u>Procedure</u>

1. Draw an egg shape on your paper.

2. Color it heavily with a dark crayon.

3. Use the tip if a paper clip to scratch a design into the crayon.

4. Cut out the egg.

5. You might draw several scratched eggs.

6. Put them in a basket that you drew on paper. On the basket, tell what the eggs are saying.

Eggs on the Internet

Using the handout on page 55, have the children visit the website listed and answer the questions. *Answers to Activity: 1.50; 2. 300-325; 3. 4; 4. 50; 5. 200*

Additional Reading

More Collections of African Folktales

Bryan, Ashley. *Lion and the Ostrich Chick: And Other African Folk Tales.* Atheneum, 1986. 87 pp. RL: 3.0. Retold folktales from many African tribes. Illustrated by the author.

Aardema, Verna. *Misoso: One Upon a Time Stories from Africa.* Alfred Knopf, 1994. 48 pp. RL: 3.0. African folktales that reveal a variety of cultures and traditions.

Steptoe, John. *Mufaro's Beautiful Daughters.* Lothrop, 1987. 32 pp. RL: 3.0. A Zimbabwe version of the classic Cinderella tale.

San Souci, Robert D. Illus. by Jerry Pinkney. *The Talking Eggs: A Folktale from the American South.* Dial, 1989. 32 pp. RL: 3.0. A southern version of the Cinderella tale with African American characters.

Berry, James. *A Thief in the Village and Other Stories.* Orchard, 1987. 148 pp. RL: 5.0. Stories about the life of the people in a Jamaican village.

"Catskinella" Guessing Game

Guess a very important thing that Catskinella did in this story. Cut the clue cards apart and lay face down on a table. Taking turns a player chooses a clue and reads it aloud. The player tries to guess from the clue what Catskinella did. If the guess is not correct the clue is placed back in the pile. The game continues until the action is guessed.

You can do this alone.	**Women do it.**	**Men do it.**
You usually do this in one room of the house.	**You need special utensils to do this.**	**You need an oven to do this.**
Sometimes this requires a recipe.	**To do this you need to follow directions.**	**You can do this at any time of day.**
Eggs are usually needed to do this.	**This is often done before a birthday.**	**You need heat to do this.**

Internet Activity

Fill in the missing number in each blank space. Guess if you do not know. Then support or deny your guesses by visiting this Internet site:

Egg Trivia: All You Ever Need to Know
http://www.enc-online.org/trivia.htm

1. In the United states 240 million hens produce _____ billion eggs each year.

2. The average hen lays _____ to _____ eggs a year.

3. A hen must eat _____ pound of feed to lay one dozen eggs.

4. One dozen extra large eggs weighs _____ ounces.

5. A mother hen turns over her egg _____ times a day.

6. There are now _____ breeds of chickens.

11

Justin and the Best Biscuits in the World

Written and Illustrated by Mildred Pitts Walter
1987 Author Award Winner

About the Book

There's nothing Justin would rather do than ride the prairie with Grandpa. Mending fences isn't a chore when followed by a meal cooked over an open fire. Justin and Grandpa eat to the songs of the blackbirds and at night Justin listens to the song of his family's history as Grandpa reads. For a city boy whose Mama and sisters are always fussing at him, there is no place Justin would rather be than Grandpa's ranch. Here is the story of a boy's struggle to make it in a man's world even though he is surrounded by women. *(Lothrop, 1986. 122 pp. Reading Level: 3.5)*

About the Author/Illustrator

Mildred Pitts Walter was born in Louisiana, taught school in California and served as an educational consultant in Colorado. Since 1969 she has been a full-time writer of children's books in which she conveys a sense of history to young readers. In addition, her picture book, *My Mama Needs Me*, helps children to cope with, what for them is a major crisis, the new baby in the house. Mrs. Walter and her husband have been active in both civil rights and world peace causes. They are the parents of two sons.

Before Reading Activity

Finish the Sentence Game

Form teams of two or three. Each team chooses one sentence starter and writes as many different endings as possible in a four minute time limit. The team with the most endings is the winner. All of the sentence starters should be related in general to the novel. Some samples appear below.

1. Living in a household of women…

2. Life on a ranch can be hard when…

3. Knowing your family's history is important because…

4. Prairie life that can be heard but not seen…

5. Finishing a task you didn't know you could do…

A Rank Order Game

Form teams of four to six. Make sentence strips like the ones below, containing something the main character does in the story (one set for each team). The team must place the strips in order from the most liked activity (as agreed upon by the team) to the least liked activity. Have the teams share their rankings to see if any of them agreed.

Listen to a good storyteller.
Ride fences with a cowboy.
Rescue a baby doe caught in a barbed wire fence.
Cook a meal over a campfire.
Take part in a pie-eating contest.
Pitch horseshoes.
Watch a rodeo cowboy ride a bull.

After Reading Activities

Questions to Think About

1. What things did Grandpa do that surprised Justin?

2. What activity with Grandpa do you think Justin liked best? Why?

3. Why did Grandpa think it was important to tell Justin the story of his family?

4. If you were Justin would you have wanted to go home when it was time? Why or why not?

5. What do you think was the most important lesson Justin learned from his Grandpa?

Famous Cowboys Research/Writing Activity

Have the children research a famous cowboy and do the simple writing assignment on page 58.

Make a Box Guitar

For each child, you will need: a shoe box; rubber bands; scissors; paper towel tube; and a pencil.

Directions

1. Cut an oval-shaped hole in the top of the box.

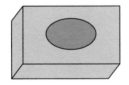

2. Stretch a few rubber bands around the box and over the hole. Put a pencil under the rubber bands on one side.

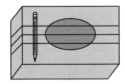

3. Tape on a paper towel tube and decorate the box.

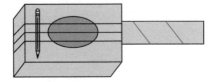

Have the children accompany themselves as they sing "Home, Home on the Range," or another familiar cowboy song.

Campfire Story Game

Sitting in a circle the first storyteller begins by reading these lines:

"It was a hot day on the trail. Buzz and Little Sis had ridden for hours searching for a water hole. The summer had been so dry that even a mosquito couldn't find enough water to drink. The horses seemed nervous and tossed their heads from one side to another. Then Buzz and Little Sis saw the reason why. Out of the bushes came ...."

The second player on the storyteller's left, continues the story, passes it clockwise, to the third player until each person in the circle has added to the tale. The last person in the circle (the one on the storyteller's right) finishes the story.

Internet Activity

Hand out the worksheet on page 59 and have the children answer the questions about rodeos and use the website provided to verify their answers.

Answers to Questions: Numbers 2, 9 and 12 are false. All other statements are true.

Additional Reading

Read About Cowboys

Pinkney, Andrea Davis. *Bill Pickett: Rodeo Ridin' Cowboy.* Harcourt Brace, 1996. 32 pp. RL: 3.0. Picture book biography of the first African American National Hall of Fame cowboy who performed in rodeos around the world.

Miller, Robert H. *Buffalo Soldiers: The Story of Emanuel Stance.* Silver Burdett, 1996. 32 pp. RL: 2.0. A picture biography of an African American hero of the wild west.

Miller, Robert H. *The Story of Nat Love.* Silver Burdett, 1994. 32 pp. RL: 2.0. Biography of a slave who became a famous wild west bronco buster.

Knowlton, Laurie K. *Why Cowboys Sleep With Their Boots On.* Pelican, 1995. 32 pp. RL: 2.0. Pesky varmints take a cowboy's wardrobe while he sleeps.

Famous Cowboys Research/Writing Activity

There have been many famous cowboys throughout history. Here are just a few:

Nat Love: A black cowboy who could outride and outshoot anyone.
Bill Pickett: A black cowboy who invented steer wrestling.
Lucille Marshall: World's lady champion in roping and tying steers.
Tom Mix: Silent-movie cowboy actor.
Roy Rogers: A singing cowboy with his horse, Trigger. Starred in movies.
Guy Weadick: Organized the first Calgary Stampede.

Find more information about two of these famous cowboys/cowgirls. Use the information in the pattern that follows.

If I were (name) _____

My home would be _____

And I'd spend my days _____

And _____

I would be really good at _____

But I wouldn't _____

Because _____ did that.

Internet Activity

Find Out about Rodeos

Answer these questions yes or no. Then support or deny your guesses by visiting this Internet site:

Britannica.com—Rodeo
http://www.britannica.com/bcom/eb/article/9/0,5716,65669+1+64024,00.html

1. _____ There are five standard rodeo events.

2. _____ In a barrel race, the rider wears a barrel.

3. _____ Cheyenne, Wyoming, claims to be the first place to hold a rodeo.

4. _____ In 1903 Bill Picket wrestled a steer to the ground, biting its upper lip in a bulldog grip.

5. _____ Lucille Marshall was called the first cowgirl.

6. _____ The Miller brothers organized one of the first Wild West shows.

7. _____ The purpose of the Rodeo Association of America is to regulate the sport.

8. _____ Calf roping and steer wrestling are timed events.

9. _____ In calf roping at least three feet must be tied together.

10. _____ In steer wrestling the wrestler must throw the steer with head and all feet in line.

11. _____ In riding events the rider is mounted before the chute is opened.

12. _____ Broncos are not trained to buck.

12
Minty

A Story of Young Harriet Tubman

Illustrated by Jerry Pinkney, Written by Alan Schroeder
1997 Illustrator Award Winner

About the Book

Young Harriet Tubman was stubborn and head-strong. She refused to listen to older, wiser heads and was considered a "problem" slave by her master. She lived on the Brodas plantation in the 1820s and was more often in trouble than not. Here is the story of a child who told Bible stories to her torn rag doll, who was sometimes too bold for her own good, and who learned from her father survival skills—how to follow the North Star, how to skin a squirrel, and how to read a tree—things that would one day help her to escape. *(Penguin Putnam, 1996. 40 pp. Reading Level: 3.0)*

About the Author

Alan Schroeder is an award-winning author whose books have received wide acclaim. His first children's book, *Ragtime Trumpie*, was a Parents Choice Award Winner, an ALA Notable Book and a Booklist Children's Editors' Choice. He also wrote *Lily and the Wooden Bowl* and *Carolina Shout*. His home is in Alameda, California.

About the Illustrator

Jerry Pinkney was born in Philadelphia and lives now in Croton-on-Hudson, New York. His books depict the individuality within a black community and his characters are portrayed as naturally as possible. Jerry Pinkney's books have received many awards and his art is shown in many galleries throughout the United States. Jerry's son Brian has followed in his father's footsteps as a children's book illustrator.

Before Reading Activity

Open Ended Sentence Starters

Before sharing *Minty: A Story of Young Harriet Tubman*, ask students to choose one of the open-ended sentence starters that follow and to finish the sentence. After hearing the story read or reading the story ask if each would finish the sentence in the same way or would they now finish it differently.

1. When a child is told by an adult to do something…
2. A really good place to be alone is…
3. Pretending can be fun when…
4. Knocking over a pitcher of cider might lead to…
5. When no one believes in your dream….
6. A field slave has a hard life because…
7. When someone destroys your most prized possession…
8. If you don't have a horse, one way to travel is…
9. An abolitionist stands for…
10. If a child finds an animal caught in a trap…
11. Skills for survival in the forest are…
12. When there is trouble, family members help by…

13. Giving up something you really want because someone else's needs are greater…

14. When you finally achieve your dream…

15. Believing in yourself means…

After Reading Activities

Questions to Think About

1. Why do you think Harriet attempted to escape even though she knew it would lead to a whipping?

2. Why did Mrs. Brody burn Harriet's doll?

3. What traits Harriet displayed as a child led her to be a successful Underground Railroad conductor?

4. Why do you think Harriet let the muskrats go rather than collecting them as she was ordered?

5. What is injustice? What examples of injustice did you find in this story?

6. Suppose that for one day Harriet were the Mistress of the plantation. How do you think she would have treated Mrs. Brody? Why?

Harriet Tubman Bio Poem

Using the handout on page 62, have the children write bio poems about Harriet Tubman.

Beastly Bookmark

The slaves on the Underground Railroad met many beasts along the way, both human and animal. Have the children make a Beastly Bookmark to remind them of the slaves' courage and determination.

For this activity, each child will need: one 3"x 5" piece of green construction paper or lightweight tagboard; crayons; marking pencils; and scissors.

Directions for Bookmark

1. Trace the pattern on heavy tagboard. Cut out.

2. Have the children trace around the pattern on green paper. With crayons or markers, have them make their own beast distinctive.

3. Cut out the beast. Add finishing touches with crayons or markers. Cut on the dotted lines.

4. To use the bookmark, clip the beast's long snout or mouth part over the book page.

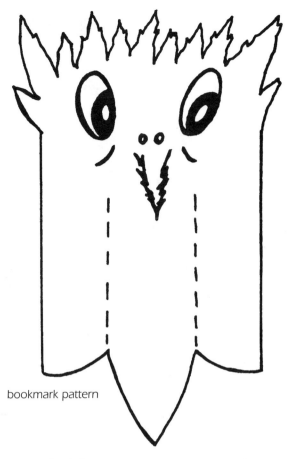

bookmark pattern

Internet Activity

Using the handout on page 63, have the children browse the sites provided and list the major accomplishments of some famous African Americans.

Additional Reading

More Tales of the Underground Railroad

Ringgold, Faith. *Aunt Harriet's Underground Railroad in the Sky.* Crown, 1992. 32 pp. RL: 2.0. Two little girls meet a train of people and retrace the steps of escaping slaves on the underground railroad.

Winter, Jeanette. *Follow the Drinking Gourd.* Knopf, 1988. 32 pp. RL: 3.0. By following directions in a song taught to them by an old sailor, runaway slaves journey north along the underground railroad to freedom.

Johnson, Delores. *Now Let Me Fly: The Story of a Slave Family.* Macmillan, 1993. 32 pp. RL: 2.0. The life of a slave as told through the eyes of one woman, captured as a child in Africa and taken to the United States.

Harriet Tubman Bio Poem

Use the bio poem model that follows to describe Harriet.

First name _____

Four traits _____

Related to _____

Cares deeply about _____

Who feels _____

Who needs _____

Who gives _____

Who would like to see _____

Resident of _____

Here is an example of a bio poem about another great African American woman.

Ida Bell Wells
First name: Ida
Four traits: intelligent, courageous, tenacious, compassionate
Related to: Lizzie and James Wells
Cares deeply about: inadequate schools for blacks
Who feels: anger when her newspaper is destroyed by a mob
Who needs: to campaign against lynching
Who gives: opinions in her newspaper column
Who would like to see: equal rights for all people
Resident of: wherever injustice took her.

Internet Activity

Surf the Internet to discover how courage and determination helped these famous African Americans to achieve fame. List the major accomplishment of each person.

Jackie Robinson www.jackie42.com/jrbio.html

_____

Mae Jemison www.lib.lsu.edu/lib/chem/display/jemison.html

_____

Harriet Tubman www.chapman.edu/students/jchall/HarrietTubman.html

_____

Sojourner Truth http://library.thinkquest.org/10320/Truth.htm

_____

Booker T. Washington http://library.thinkquest.org/10320/Washngtn.htm

_____

Rosa Parks www.worldbook.com/fun/aajourny/html/bh088.html

_____

Jesse Owens www.worldbook.com/fun/aajourny/html/bh069.html

_____

Thurgood Marshall www.worldbook.com/fun/aajourny/html/bh140.html

_____

George Washington Carver http://library.thinkquest.org/10320/Carver.htm

_____

Frederick Douglass http://library.thinkquest.org/10320/Douglass.htm

_____

13
Mirandy and Brother Wind

Illustrated by Jerry Pinkney, Written by Patricia McKissack
1989 Illustrator Award Winner

About the Book

"Whoever catch the Wind can make him do their bidding," Ma Dear tells Mirandy who wants the wind to be her partner at the junior cakewalk. But catching the wind proves to be a formidable task. Mirandy asks Grandmama Beasley and all her neighbors how to go about capturing Brother Wind, but no one has the answer. She tries putting black pepper out and throwing a quilt on the Wind. She learns a conjure from Mis Poinsettia and follows all the directions but finds Brother Wind just laughing at her from the other side of a tree. Finally she locks the Wind in the barn. At the cakewalk Mirandy finds the girls making fun of her friend Ezel and tells them that he is to be her partner and that there is no doubt the two of them will win that cake. And win they do, with Mirandy wearing Mis Poinsettia's scarves and Ezel standing tall with his head high. *(Knopf, 1988. 32 pp. Reading Level: 3.0)*

About the Author

Patricia C. McKissack grew up in Nashville, Tennessee where she lived with caring grandparents who gave her a love of books and reading. She remembers many nights reading aloud to her grandfather and hearing her grandmother's stories. Her love of literature led her to a teaching profession and from there to editing children's books for Concordia Publishing Company. She and her husband, Fred have their own company, All Writing Services, and often team in the writing of children's books, both fiction and non-fiction.

About the Illustrator

Jerry Pinkney was born in Philadelphia and lives now in Croton-on-Hudson, New York. His books depict the individuality within a black community and his characters are portrayed as naturally as possible, Jerry Pinkney's books have received many awards and his art is shown in many galleries throughout the United States. Jerry's son Brian has followed in his father's footsteps as a children's book illustrator.

Before Reading Activity

What Do You Think?

Have the children answer yes or no to the following questions. After hearing the story, see if they feel differently about any of their answers.

1. It is possible to catch the wind.

2. No one wants to dance with a clumsy dancer.

3. People go to a cakewalk to see cakes walk.

4. Black pepper will make the wind sneeze.

5. A strong wind will frighten hens in a barn.

After Reading Activities

Discussing the Story

After reading *Mirandy and Brother Wind*, use these questions to start a discussion about the story.

1. List as many words as you can to describe Mirandy. Explain which one word in your list best describes her.

2. How do you know that this story took place almost 100 years ago?

3. Which girl did Ezel want most to be his partner, Mirandy or Orlinda? Why do you think so?

4. Do you think Mirandy should have asked Mis Poinsettia for help knowing that her parents did not approve of conjure?

5. Why do you think Mirandy finally chose Ezel as her partner rather than Brother Wind?

Sing a Mirandy Song

Sing the following song to the tune of "My Bonnie Lies Over the Ocean"

> The wind ran away from Mirandy
> It climbed up and hid in a tree
> But she was determined to catch him
> For her cakewalk partner to be.
>
> Swoosh, Swoosh, Swish, Swish
> The wind twirls around
> See him bow and prance
> Swoosh, Swoosh, Swish, Swish
> The Wind with Mirandy won't dance.
>
> Mirandy locked Wind in the hen house
> Then heard words about her good friend
> So she and Ezel won the cakewalk
> And that's how this story will end.

I Have, Who Has Game

Cut the cards on page 66 apart and give one card to each of ten students. The student who has the card with * * * reads the "Who Has" question from the card. The student holding the card with the answer reads "I Have" and the answer. Then that student reads the "Who Has" question from his or her card. The game continues until all cards have been read.

Internet Activities

The worksheet on page 67 provides two Internet activities focused on the wind.

Answers for The Wind–Friend or Enemy: Friend: cools the home, sails boats, lulls infants to sleep. Enemy: whips sailboats toward rocks, hurricanes destroy homes, slams shutters, dampens picnic plans.

Answer for Why Does the Wind Blow?: The correct order is 1, 4, 2, 6, 5, 3.

Additional Reading

More Stories About the Wind

Lasky, Katherine. *Gates of the Wind.* Harcourt Brace, 1995. 32 pp. RL: 2.0. An old woman and the blowing wind reach a compromise on a mountain peak.

Martin, Jr., Bill. *Old Devil Wind.* Harcourt Brace, 1993. 32 pp. RL: 2.0. A house and its inhabitants are rattled by a great wind.

de Paola, Tomie. *The Wind the Sun.* Silver Burdett, 1994. 32 pp. RL: 2.0. A retelling of the Aesop's fable about the contest between the wind and the sun.

Hutchins, Pat. *The Wind Blew.* Viking, 1986. 32 pp. RL: 2.0. People chase items in the air that the wind has stolen from them.

Rydell, Katy. *The Wind Says Goodnight.* Houghton-Mifflin, 1994. 32 pp. RL: 1.0. A child can't sleep until all of nature quiets down.

I Have, Who Has
Game Cards

I Have Mirandy and Ezel won the cakewalk. * * * **Who Has** Who did Mirandy want for a cake-walk partner?	**I Have** Mirandy wanted Brother Wind for her cakewalk partner. **Who Has** Why did Mirandy get black pepper?
I Have Mirandy got black pepper to make the wind sneeze. **Who Has** Why did Mirandy visit Mis Poinsettia?	**I Have** Mirandy visited Mis Poinsettia to ask for help in capturing he wind. **Who Has** What did Mis Poinsettia **give** Mirandy?
I Have Mis Poinsettia gave Mirandy advice and see-through scarves. **Who Has** Why did Mirandy put cider in the crock bottle?	**I Have** Mirandy put cider in the bottle to tempt Brother Wind. **Who Has** Why was Mirandy moping on the front porch swing?
I Have Mirandy was moping because she couldn't catch the wind. **Who Has** Why did Mirandy think the wind could not get out of the barn?	**I Have** Mirandy thought the wind could not get out of the barn because father had stuffed all the cracks. **Who Has** Where was the cakewalk held?
I Have The cakewalk was held in the schoolhouse. **Who Has** How did the girls at the cakewalk treat Ezel?	**I Have** The girls at the cakewalk made fun of Ezel. **Who Has** Who won the cakewalk?

Internet Activities

Activity 1: The Wind–Friend or Enemy?

Place an F before the phrases that show the wind is a friend and an E before the phrases that show the wind is an enemy. Visit this website to check your answers and to read about other activities you can do with wind.

> **Franklin Institute Online—Wind**
> http://sln.fi.edu/tfi/units/energy/wind.html

_____ cools the home   _____ hurricanes destroy homes

_____ whips sailboats toward rocks   _____ lulls infants to sleep

_____ sends kites into the sky   _____ slams shutters

_____ moves sailboats across the waves   _____dampens picnic plans

Activity 2: Why Does the Wind Blow?

Place these sentences in order to tell why the wind blows. Check your order on this website:

> **National Geographic.com—Amazing Facts**
> http://www.nationalgeographic.com/world/amfacts/amaz6.html

1. As the sun warms the earth's surface, the atmosphere warms too.

2. Other places receive indirect rays, so the climate is colder.

3. This movement of air is what makes the wind blow.

4. Some parts of the earth receive direct rays from the sun all year and are always warm.

5. Then cool air moves in and replaces rising warm air.

6. Warm air, which weighs less than cool air, rises.

From *Celebrating the Coretta Scott King Awards*. Copyright © 2000 by Nancy Polette. (Alleyside Press, 2000)

14

Mufaro's Beautiful Daughters

An African Tale

Written and Illustrated by John Steptoe

1988 Illustrator Award Winner

About the Book

Long ago in Africa, Mufaro had two beautiful daughters. Manyara was selfish and greedy and teased her sister Nyasha, who was kind and loving. Manyara spent her days in a bad temper, Nyasha spent her days tending her garden and singing to her friend, the little garden snake who lived there.

A message arrives in the village from the Great King who is looking for a wife. Mufaro decides that both his daughters will go to appear before the king. Manyara is pleased and is sure she will be chosen queen. Nyasha would prefer to remain in the village tending her garden and looking after her father.

In order to be first, Manyara sneaks off into the night ignoring a hungry boy, and an old woman's advice. Nyasha gives food to the boy and sunflower seeds to the old woman. When she reaches the city she finds her frightened sister who has seen the king and describes him as a monster snake with five heads.

When Nyasha enters the chamber she finds her friend, the garden snake, who changes into the shape of the king. He tells Nyasha that he was the garden snake, the boy and the old woman and asks her to be his wife. (Lothrop, 1987. 32 pp. Reading Level: 3.5)

The Background of the Book

The author states that *Mufaro's Beautiful Daughters* was adapted from a folktale collected by G. M. Theal and published in 1895. The locale of the story is the country of Zimbabwe. In southeastern Zimbabwe, in 1870, European explorers came upon an impressive ruined city, which they believed to be the biblical city of Ophir—the site of King Solomon's mines. It is this city and the surrounding countryside that served as the basis for the illustrations in the book.

About the Author/Illustrator

John Steptoe was born in Brooklyn, New York, in 1950. He amazed the children's book world by having his first picture book, *Stevie*, published when he was only nineteen-years-old. This was the first of many award-winning books John Steptoe created for children. He chose his career at a very early age, knowing that his goal in life was to create picture books for African American children ... the kinds of books that he rarely saw as a child. John's son, Javaka, has followed in his father's footsteps, creating award-winning picture books of his own. John Steptoe died in 1989 at the age of 39.

Before Reading Activity

What Will You Predict?

Tell the children that some parts of this African Cinderella story will be different from the Cinderella tale with which they are familiar. Before hearing the story, have them predict the correct answer to each of the following multiple choice questions.

1. The African Cinderella has: (a) one sister (b) two stepsisters (c) three stepsisters

2. She lives in: (a) a large house (b) a village (c) a palace

3. She is helped by: (a) a snake (b) a fairy godmother (c) a lion

4. She is taken to the king by: (a) magic coach (b) her father (c) an elephant

5. She wanted to: (a) visit the king (b) tend her garden

6. In the end she marries: (a) a king (b) a rich man (c) a prince

Answers: 1. a; 2. b; 3. a; 4. b; 5. b; 6. a.

After Reading Activities

Discussing the Story

Give one of the following questions to each of five groups of students to discuss for five minutes. At the end of the discussion time one student from each group reports to the class.

1. List all the ways that you know that Manyara was greedy and selfish, and Nyasha was kind and good.

2. Why do you think Nyasha consented to marry the king even though she wanted to stay in her village and tend her garden?

3. What do you think the hungry boy, the old woman and the man with his head under his arm represented? Why were they included in the story?

4. Suppose that Nyasha had not met the snake in the garden. How would the story change?

5. List all the ways you can that this story is like the story of Cinderella.

Be a Designer

Using the handout on page 71 and have the children decorate their own outfit for an African king.

A Library Game: Guess Who You Are!

1. Make signs or label pictures for the following:

   Mufaro, The Old Woman, Man With Head Under Arm, Manyara, Nyasha, The Hungry Boy, Garden Snake, Laughing Trees, The King

2. The sign or labeled picture is pinned or taped to the back of a student.

3. Students walk around and talk to each other as if each was the famous person indicated by the sign.

   Example
   The Laughing Trees might hear the following:

   "My, you certainly are tall."
   "It must be hard to travel without two legs."
   "Your best friends must be the sun and the rain ."

4. When a student guesses correctly who he or she is, the sign is taken off and held in the hand.

5. Students wearing signs can also ask others questions about the character they are supposed to be but their questions cannot use the name of any character. All questions must be answered by only yes or no.

   Example

   "Do I talk a lot?" (no)
   "Is my favorite color green?" (yes)

Internet Activity

Using the worksheet on page 72, have the children visit the website on Zimbabwe and do the simple writing assignment.

Additional Reading

More Cinderella Stories from Around the World

Climo, Shirley. *The Egyptian Cinderella.* HarperCollins, 1989. 32 pp. RL: 3.0. An Egyptian slave girl is eventually chosen by the Pharaoh to be his queen.

Climo, Shirley. *The Irish Cinderlad.* HarperCollins, 1996. 32 pp. RL: 3.0. A poor boy, belittled by his stepmother and stepsisters, rescues a princess in distress.

Climo, Shirley. *The Korean Cinderella.* HarperCollins, 1993. 32 pp. RL: 3.0. A Cinderella tale in which Pear Blossom must perform three impossible tasks.

San Souci, Robert. *The Talking Eggs.* Dial, 1989. 32 pp. RL: 3.0. Blanche, following the instructions of an old woman, gets riches and her selfish sister gets none.

Louie, Ai-Ling. *Yeh Shen: A Cinderella Story from China.* Putnam, 1982. 32 pp. RL: 3.0. A young Chinese girl overcomes the wickedness of her stepsisters to become the bride of a prince.

Be a Designer

Color in the clothing with your own designs for this African king.

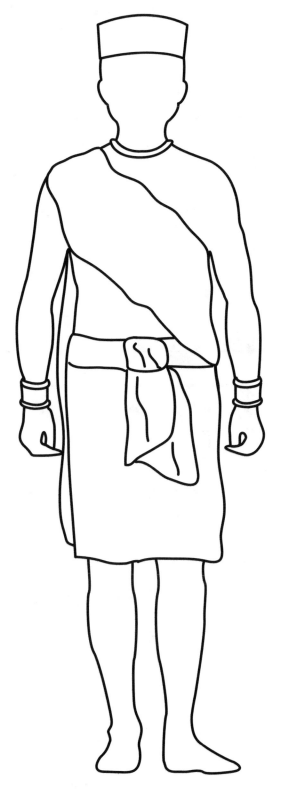

Internet Activity

Visit this Zimbabwe website. Read the description and look at the beautiful photographs of this country. Write about Zimbabwe using the pattern that follows.

Geographia—Zimbabwe
http://www.geographia.com/zimbabwe/

Let's go to long ago places and see the earth's many faces.

We Will See

1. _____
2. _____
3. _____
4. _____
5. _____
6. _____

But That's Not All

1. _____
2. _____
3. _____
4. _____
5. _____
6. _____

Where Am I? _____ (*answer*)

15

My Mama Needs Me

Illustrated by Pat Cummings,
Written by Mildred Pitts Walter
1984 Illustrator Award Winner

About the Book

When a new baby comes an older child might not only feel rejected but not needed. This is precisely Jason's problem as he wants so much to be needed by his mama to help with his new little sister. It seems, however, that all new babies do is eat and sleep. Jason refuses cookies from a neighbor, games with his friends and watching ducks at the pond just in case his mama needs him. But each time he checks, he doesn't seem to be needed at all. At last the baby is awake, and Mama asks Jason's help in bathing her. And most important of all, Mama shows Jason how much she needs him, especially his hugs. *(Lothrop, 1983. 32 pp. Reading Level: 2.0)*

About the Author

Mildred Pitts Walter was born in Louisiana, taught school in California and served as an educational consultant in Colorado. Since 1969 she has been a full-time writer of children's books in which she conveys a sense of history to young readers. Her picture book, *My Mama Needs Me*, helps children to cope with, what for them is a major crisis, the new baby in the house. Mrs. Walter and her husband have been active in both civil rights and world peace causes. They are the parents of two sons.

About the Illustrator

Pat Cummings was born in Chicago and now lives with her husband in New York City. As the daughter of a military family she traveled widely, observing carefully all that she saw in each new place. Her art ability helped her to make friends even though the friendships would not be long lasting because of the frequent moves. Her unique illustrations show her love for freedom and use of imagination.

Before Reading Activities

Finish the Sentence

Divide the group into pairs. Give each child a sheet containing the five sentence starters below and have them write their answers. Then have them compare their endings with their partner's. Were any endings the same? Were any different? Ask the children why they think some of the answers were different. (This activity can be done orally with younger children not working with partners.)

1. Having a new baby in the house is _____.

2. It is good to feel needed because _____.

3. One thing a friendly neighbor would do is _____.

4. The best thing to have for dinner is _____.

5. One of the best things to do for a parent is _____.

Vocabulary Exercise

Make cards containing the following words. Have the children hold up two words that go together and tell why.

Words for Cards

mama	baby	Jason	slept
cookies	sister	tiptoed	silence
laughed	snuggle	crying	wiggled
bassinet	ducks	pond	bathe

After Reading Activities

Discussing the Story

Assign one of the following questions to each of five small groups of students. Give sufficient time for each group to discuss the question. At the end of the discussion time one person from each group reports to the class the main ideas of the discussion.

1. How did Jason feel about having a new baby sister?

2. Why did Jason tell everyone that his mother needed him?

3. Suppose that Jason had stayed to feed the ducks. How might the story change?

4. What if Jason's mother had brought home twins? Would she have needed Jason more then?

5. Why did Jason's mother let him help bathe the baby when she could have done it by herself?

Story Strips

Place each of the following events from the story on a strip of paper or poster board. Give one to each of six students. The students line up in the correct order and each reads his or her strip to tell the story.

1. Jason went to his backyard.

2. Jason saw the ducks on the pond.

3. The new baby arrives.

4. Jason gave his mama the hug she needed.

5. Jason watched mama feed the baby.

6. Jason helped mama bathe the baby.

Correct order: 3,1,5,2,6,4

Let's Sing

Using words in the story, sing this song to the tune of "Hush, Little Baby." Have the children help you make up additional verses.

> Hush, little baby, don't you cry,
> Jason's gonna sing you a lullaby.
> And if that lullaby don't suit,
> Jason's gonna bring you some tasty fruit.
> And if that fruit should be too green,
> Jason's gonna bring you a lima bean.
> And if that lima been should sprout,
> Jason's gonna bring you some sauerkraut.
> And if that sauerkraut won't keep,
> Jason will sing the baby to sleep.

Internet Activity

Visit the "Kids in the Kitchen" site and have your group make up their own recipes. A handout appears on page 75.

Additional Reading

A Baby in the House

Morris, Ann. *The Baby Book.* Silver Burdett, 1995. 32 pp. RL: 2.0. A multicultural look at babies around the world.

Winter, Susan A. *A Baby Just Like Me.* Dorling Kindersley, 1994. 32 pp. RL: 2.0. A sensitive look at sibling relationships.

Steptoe, John. *Baby Says.* Morrow, 1992. 32 pp. RL: 1.0. A baby and his big brother figure out how to get along.

de Paola, Tomie. *The Baby Sister.* Putnam, 1996. 32 pp. RL: 1.0. Tommy and his Nana start to appreciate each other when his mom and baby sister come home.

Curtis, Jamie Lee. *When I Was Little.* HarperCollins, 1993. 32 pp. RL: 2.0. A spirited little girl proves she's no longer a baby.

Internet Activity

Mrs. Luby uncovered a plate of spicy brown cookies and offered them to Jason. Jason knew Mrs. Luby was a good cook, but he could not stay to eat cookies. He said his mama needed him.

Suppose Jason were to help his mother by fixing dessert for dinner. For easy recipes he could go to this Internet site:

> **Kids Kitchen**
> http://www.scoreone.com/kids_kitchen/index.htm

Choose from Major Messes: Recipes that make the most mess but taste the best; Munchies: Quick and easy to make and taste good too; or Sweet and Sticky: The most tasty delightful sweets that can be made in minutes.

If you prefer, create your own recipe. Tell Jason how to cook the chicken his mother has taken out of the refrigerator.

First:_____

_____

_____

Add:_____

_____

_____

Next: _____

_____

_____

Cook: (*tell where and for how long*) _____

_____

_____

16
Nathaniel Talking

Illustrated by Jan Spivey Gilchrist, Written by Eloise Greenfield

1989 Illustrator Award Winner

About the Book

Nathaniel B. Free is a spunky, spirited nine-year-old poet who raps and rhymes about his world, from what it's like to be nine, to his education, missing his mama, making friends, mis-behaving, his daddy, his aunt and his future. Along with a fine intellect, Nathaniel is playful, curious and enthusiastic and he shares with candor his thoughts about the world and his place in it. *(Black Butterfly Children's Press, 1988. 32 pp. Reading Level: 3.0)*

About the Author

Eloise Greenfield is the author of more than twenty books for children. Her biographies, fiction and poetry have received numerous awards for excellence including the first Carter G. Woodson Award, the Jane Addams Children's Book Award and the Hope S. Dean Award for her body of work. Ms. Greenfield has taught creative writing in Washington, D.C., schools as an artist-in-education for the D.C. Commission on the Arts and Humanities. She was born in North Carolina but spent most of her life in Washington, D.C.

About the Illustrator

Jan Spivey Gilchrist, a native Chicagoan, received her master's in painting from the University of Northern Iowa. She has taught art in the public schools of Illinois and Massachusetts but now devotes her time solely to illustrating. She has received numerous awards and commissions for her work. She lives in suburban Chicago with her husband and two children.

Before Reading Activities

Would You Rather: Choices to Think About

Copy the following statements onto cards or poster board. Have the children make choices and share them with the group. Ask the group why different people might make different choices.

Would you rather:
Rap a poem
Walk with friends
Make a new friend

Would you rather:
Know everything about everything
Think about good things
Stay after school

Would you rather:
Fight a bully
Spin a yo-yo
Sing the blues

Would you rather:
Talk to pigeons
Dance to music
Play a guitar

Make a Prediction

Have the group name two reasons why the following things might happen.

1. Nine-year-old friends walk together all over the neighborhood.

2. The young boy went into his room to hide.

3. A girl puffed out her cheeks and made a funny face.

4. A boy has to stay after school.

5. Two boys began to fight.

After Reading Activities

Discussing the Book

Work in small groups with each group taking one question to discuss. At the end of the discussion time, one member from each group reports on his or her group's ideas.

1. Why was Nathaniel so proud to be walking with his friends? Do you think nine is old enough to walk with friends in a big city neighborhood? To walk alone?

2. What did Nathaniel's uncle mean when he said "You going to get past this pain"?

3. Can parents get mad and still love their children? Explain your answer.

4. What are some good ways to make friends if you are new in a school?

5. Why did Nathaniel say he was stupid to fight? List some ways problems can be solved without fighting.

6. How do you know that Nathaniel greatly admires his father? How could Nathaniel show his father that he admires him?

7. Why does Nathaniel think that his aunt does not understand about love?

8. What does it mean to have the weight of the world on your shoulders? What might cause you to feel this way?

Venn Diagram

Using the Venn Diagram on page 78, have the children compare themselves to Nathaniel.

Internet Activity

Using the worksheet on page 79, have the children think about various quotes and proverbs, and how they might relate to the characters and situations in *Nathaniel Talking*.

Additional Reading

Stories About Growing Up

Johnson, Angela. *The Aunt in the House.* Harcourt Brace, 1996. 32 pp. RL: 2.0. An interracial family welcomes the arrival of their aunt.

Clifton, Lucille. *Everett Anderson's Year.* Holt, 1992. 32 pp. RL: 1.0. A year in the life of a young African American boy who lives in the city.

Eisenberg, Phyllis Rose. *You're My Nikki.* Simon & Schuster, 1995. 32 pp. RL: 2.0. Nikki need reassurance that her mother won't forget her when she goes out to work.

Miles, Calvin. *Calvin's Christmas Wish.* Harcourt Brace, 1993. 32 pp. RL: 2.0. An African American boy learns about the real meaning of Christmas.

Cummings, Pat. *Jimmy Lee Did It.* HarperCollins, 1995. 32 pp. RL: 2.0. An imaginary boy is blamed for everything Artie does wrong.

Venn Diagram

Compare yourself and Nathaniel. How are you alike and how are you different?

About Me   **About Nathaniel**

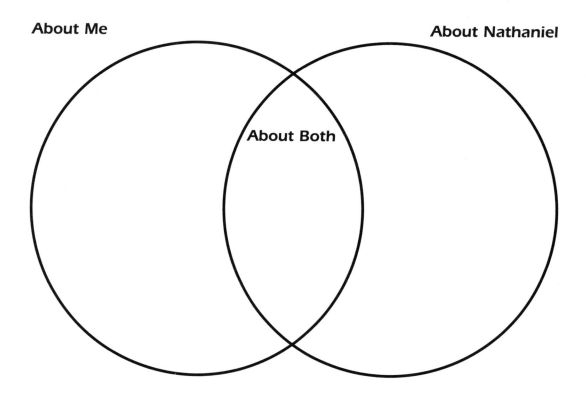

About Both

Finish this sentence.

The one thing I would most like to do with Nathaniel is

_____

_____

Internet Activity

Visit the Quoteland website below, click on topics and choose "friends". Write the quote here with which Nathaniel would most agree.

_____

_____

Quoteland
http://www.quoteland.com

Proverbs: Wise Sayings!

A proverb is a wise saying that can often be applied to many situations. Look at these proverbs and decide which would apply to the situations below. Write the proverb that would apply and tell why.

Don't cry over spilt milk.   Let sleeping dogs lie.

Every cloud has a silver lining.   If the shoe fits, wear it.

Two wrongs don't make a right.   Actions speak louder than words.

Look before you leap.   He who hesitates is lost.

Where there's smoke there's fire.   Beggars can't be choosers.

A watched pot never boils.

1. Proverb: _____
   applies to Nathaniel getting into a fight
   because _____

   _____

2. Proverb: _____
   applies to Aunt Lavinia who won't come to visit
   because _____

   _____

17

The Patchwork Quilt

Illustrated by Jerry Pinkney, Written by Valerie Flourney
1986 Illustrator Award Winner

About the Book

Tanya's Grandma liked to sit in her favorite chair by the window where the light shone in. She needed good light to work on her patchwork quilt, made from bits and pieces of her children's and grandchildren's lives. The quilt was to be filled with good memories. There were patches from brother Ted's shirt, Tanya's halloween costume, Mama's Christmas dress and so many more … each recalling a good time in the lives of the family. But when Grandma became ill and could no longer work on the quilt, it was only half finished. Then Tanya and Ted helped to cut the squares while Mama sewed. It took a long time, all through the winter and into the spring. The quilt was almost finished. Then Tanya remembered a missing piece, the most important piece of all. Something of Grandma's had to be part of the quilt and Tanya knew just what it should be. When the quilt was finally finished, Tanya receives another surprise. The quilt is hers to treasure for a lifetime. *(Dial, 1985. 32 pp. Reading Level: 3.5)*

About the Author

Valerie Flournoy is the author of another book about Tanya and her grandmother, *Tanya's Reunion,* which is based on Ms. Flournoy's memories of her first visit to a relative's farm. She also wrote *The Best Time of Day* and *The Twins Strike Back*. The author devotes her time to writing and speaking to groups of children around the country. A graduate of William Smith College, she lives in her family home in Palmyra, New Jersey, with her twin sister, Vanessa.

About the Illustrator

Jerry Pinkney, a three time Caldecott Honor Book artist, is a prolific illustrator of children's books as well as a designer of postage stamps and record album covers. He is the only artist ever to have won three Coretta Scott King Awards for Illustration and two Coretta Scott King Honor Awards. He was born in Philadelphia and grew up in a black community there where he observed the great diversity in appearance and talents among people. He portrays this individuality in his illustrations with great love and admiration. His illustrations for *Mirandy and Brother Wind* received the Caldecott Honor Award and the Coretta Scott King Illustrator Award. He also received the Coretta Scott King Illustrator Award for *Half a Moon and One Whole Star* and *The Patchwork Quilt.*

Before Reading Activities

Rank Order

Working in groups of four or five, have the children rank order these items of clothing from the one the group would most like to wear to the one least liked. The group must agree on and be ready to share the reasons for their rankings.

____ Gap t-shirt   ____ leather jacket

____ Nike shoes   ____ wide leg jeans

____ Levis   ____ Halloween costume

Sentence Starters

Have each child choose one of the following sentence starters to complete, and add two more sentences about the topic. Have them share their sentences with the class.

1. A good memory to have is…

2. Making a quilt takes time because…

3. Dressing up on Halloween can be…

4. When someone in the family is ill…

5. One year is a long time to…

6. The arrival of autumn means…

7. When everything is covered with snow…

After Reading Activities

Discussing the Story

1. Why did Mother at first feel that Grandma should not be making a quilt?

2. How did Grandma show that remembering "the old ways" was important?

3. Why was it important to Grandma that her quilt be a "masterpiece"?

4. Mama pleaded with Grandma to move away from the drafty window but she would not move. Why?

5. Why did the rest of the family work on the quilt when Grandma became ill? Why didn't they wait for her to finish it when she got better?

6. Do you think Tanya will get in trouble for cutting off a piece of Grandma's old quilt? Why or why not?

7. Why do you think the quilt was given to Tanya rather than her mother?

Make a Story Quilt Square

Directions for this craft appear on page 82.

Christmas at Tanya's House

Using the worksheet on page 83, have the children list things they might find at Tanya's house at Christmas.

Internet Activities

A worksheet with different Internet activities focusing on quilts appears on page 83.

Additional Reading

Quilt Stories

Hopkinson, Deborah. *Sweet Clara and the Freedom Quilt.* Knopf, 1993. 32 pp. RL: 2.0. Taken from a true incident, this is the story of a young slave who uses a quilt as a map to the underground railroad.

Jonas, Ann. *Quilt.* Morrow, 1984. 32 pp. RL: 1.0. A child's quilt contains bits of material from former belongings and comforts her on the way to sleep.

Cobb, Mary. *Quilt Block History of Pioneer Days.* Millbrook, 1995. 48 pp. RL: 3.0. Easy paper craft quilt projects showing how the lives of the pioneers were reflected in the quilts they made.

Johnston, Tony. Illus. by Tomie de Paola. *The Quilt Story.* Putnam, 1985. 32 pp. RL: 3.0. Two little girls, generations apart, love the same family quilt.

Make a Story Quilt Square

In *The Patchwork Quilt*, each square in the quilt helped a family member to remember a special time in their lives. The square was made from something the person wore. Create a story quilt square by having the nine windows tell a story.

What You Need

One sheet each of white paper and colored paper (8½ x 11" or 11 x 14") scissors, glue, crayons

What to Do

1. Fold your colored paper in half and then in half again.

2. Make three two-side cuts on each fold.

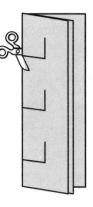

3. Open your paper. Fold back each cut to make a window.

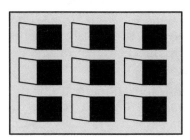

4. Glue the white paper under the colored along the edges.

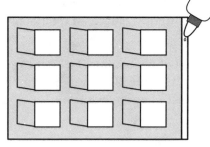

5. Open one window at a time. Draw and color one thing in each window to tell a story.

Christmas at Tanya's House

At Christmas Papa said he had never felt so much happiness in a house. Pretend you are a visitor in Tanya's house at Christmas. Fill in the chart with things you might find.

Sights	Sounds	Smells	Tastes	Feelings

Use some of the things you listed to describe Tanya's house at Christmas in a five senses poem by completing the pattern below.

Tanya's house looks like_____

It sounds like_____

It smells like_____

It tastes like_____

It makes Tanya feel _____

Internet Activities

Activity 1

Visit this website to discover how your class can send photos and drawings of your community to be added to a Global Village Internet Quilt.

International Quilt Project
http://www.ccsd.net/community/quiltproject/index.html

Activity 2

Visit this website for titles and descriptions of many other story books about quilts. Find and read one of the books and review the book for your class.

Quilt Stories
http://www.ttsw.com/FAQS/BooksChildrenFAQ.html

Activity 3

Design a quilt square that tells something about you. Draw your design on a piece of 8½ x 11" paper. If others in your group design squares, these can be pinned to a bulletin board for a paper quilt. Make a sketch of your design below.

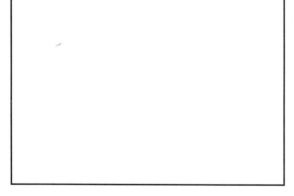

For interesting quilt designs, see this website:

Womenfolk.com—Vintage Gallery
http://www.womenfolk.com/grandmothers/gallery.htm

18
The People Could Fly
American Black Folktales
Written by Virginia Hamilton,
Illustrated by Leo & Diane Dillon
Knopf, 1985 ■ 1986 Author Award Winner

About the Book

Here are tales where the wily Bruh Rabbit outwits larger and stronger animals. There are all tales filled with riddles and laughter. Included too are spine-tingling ghost tales as well as tales of freedom including both true slave narratives and fantasy escapes in the title tale, "The People Could Fly."

Activities are included for the first and last tales in the collection. "He Lion, Bruh Bear, and Bruh Rabbit" tells the tale of Lion who delights in scaring all the other animals with his terrible roar. The animals take their problem to Bruh Bear and Bruh Rabbit who go to talk to Lion. At first Lion insists he will roar when he pleases, until Bruh Rabbit leads him to Man, with his exploding stick. After his meeting with Man, Lion does not roar nearly as loud.

"The People Could Fly" is a fantasy escape tale of slaves who work in the fields from sun up till sun down. Those who don't work fast enough get the whip. Even Sarah and her babe get the whip. When she is unable to rise she appeals to old Toby who tells her that "The time is come. Go, as you know how to go." With her child in her arms, Sarah is the first to rise free in the air and fly away. The following day with old Toby's help, all the slaves join hands and follow her....all, that is, except the slaves who cannot fly. But it is these who keep the story alive for many years to come. *(Knopf, 1985. 178 pp. Reading Level: 5.0)*

About the Author

Virginia Hamilton grew up on a farm in rural Ohio, the youngest of five children. Many of her books reflect her own life: growing up in an extended family, her closeness to her grandparents with their fabulous storehouse of black legend, a love for the small town Midwest, and the lives and relationships of the people who live there. Ms. Hamilton has included among her many awards and honors the following: the 1975 Newbery Medal for *M. C. Higgins, The Great* and a Newbery Honor Book Award and Coretta Scott King Award for *Sweet Whispers, Brother Rush*. Ms. Hamilton lives with her husband, poet Arnold Adoff, in Ohio.

About the Illustrators

Leo and Diane Dillon were awarded the Caldecott Medal in two consecutive years. They graduated from the Parsons School of Design and for many years were on the faculty of the School of Visual Arts. hey live in Brooklyn, New York, with their artist son, Lee.

Before Reading Activities

Problem Solving Activity for "He Lion, Bruh Bear and Bruh Rabbit"

Ask the group the question, "How can you make a lion stop roaring?" Have them list their ideas in a

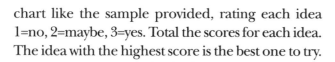

chart like the sample provided, rating each idea 1=no, 2=maybe, 3=yes. Total the scores for each idea. The idea with the highest score is the best one to try.

Ideas	Fast	Safe	Low Cost?	Will Work?	Total
Give him meat.	2	2	1	2	7

sample chart

Word Charades Game for "The People Could Fly"

Divide the group into teams of four to six players. Each team leader receives a list of five words from the story to act out for his or her team. The team guessing all the words in the shortest time is the winner. Use the following words for your lists.

magic	sea	starving	foot
gate	skin	sad	bird
wings	baby	cry	trees
ship	work	arms	fence
slave	field	whisper	breeze

After Reading Activities

Questions to Think About for "He Lion, Bruh Bear and Bruh Rabbit"

1. Why do you think Lion had to make so much noise?

2. Why weren't the small animals happy about the noise? Wouldn't they always want to know where Lion was in order to stay out of his way?

3. Rabbit was a small animal. Why wasn't he afraid of Lion?

4. Why did Rabbit tell Lion that the very old man was not a man?

5. Why did Lion decide to be more peaceable at the end of the story?

A Trickster Tale Logic Puzzle for "He Lion, Bruh Bear and Bruh Rabbit"

Using the clues and chart provided on page 87, have the children figure out the actions of the different characters.

Answers: Bear: *cherries–river; Fox: berries–burrow; Rabbit: bark–woods; Wolf: mouse–field*

Questions to Think About for "The People Could Fly"

1. What is injustice? Give examples from the story.

2. How would the story change if Toby were not a character?

3. Why do you think some of the slaves could fly and others could not?

4 . Why did the overseer refuse to believe what he saw?

5. Do you think the people really flew? Why or why not?

About Feelings Activity for "The People Could Fly"

A worksheet for this "color by letter" activity can be found on page 88.

Additional Reading

More African Folktales

Rosales, Melodye. *Leola and the Honeybears.* Scholastic, 1999. 32 pp. RL: 3.0. An African American retelling of a classic tale. Leola wanders into the forest and encounters frightening Ol' Mister Weasel, surprises the Honeybear family and learns an important lesson about strangers.

Rojany, Lisa. *The Magic Feather.* Troll, 1995. 32 pp. RL: 2.0. A young girl sets out to find a magic feather to recapture the light.

McDermott, Gerald. *The Magic Tree.* Holt, 1994. 32 pp. RL: 2.0. An African tale about twins and the secret of a magic tree.

Myers, Walter Dean. Illus. by Ashley Bryan. *The Story of the Three Kingdoms.* HarperCollins, 1995. 32 pp. RL: 3.0. Original fable about how people came to live peacefully with nature.

A Trickster Tale Logic Puzzle

The slaves created animal tales in which the animals behaved like people. Bruh Rabbit was a favorite character and since he was small and weak, the storyteller made him smart, tricky and clever. While he sometimes got in trouble, he often won out over the larger animals.

In the puzzle below Rabbit is looking for something to eat and trying not to be dinner for Bruh Bear, Bruh Fox or Bruh Wolf. Each of them finds something to eat and luckily Bruh Rabbit is not on the menu. After they eat, each goes to a different place.

Find out what each animal found to eat and what they did after they had eaten.

Clues

The wolf wanted rabbit for dinner, but he settled for a small rodent.

No animal ate food or went to a place which started with the same letter as his name.

The fox took his fruit to his burrow.

The bear lumbered down to the water after he had eaten.

	Bear	Berries	Cherries	Mouse	Burrow	Field	River	Woods
Bear								
Fox								
Rabbit								
Wolf								

About Feelings

In "The People Could Fly" there were many feelings expressed, fear, anger, sadness, and joy were a few.

Feelings and emotions are often expressed with colors such as the blacks and grays used by the Dillons to express the feelings of the slaves. Fill in the parts of the collage with the colors that correspond with each of the letters listed below. Each letter represents an emotion or feeling.

L (love)- red
S (sadness)-blue
H (happiness)-yellow
C (contentment)-flesh or tan

E (envy)-green
P (peacefulness-white
A (anger)-silver or gold

Now draw your own picture of how you feel when you are sad, happy or angry. Use the colors that make you feel the emotion you are drawing.

From *Celebrating the Coretta Scott King Awards*. Copyright © 2000 by Nancy Polette. (Alleyside Press, 2000)

19

Tar Beach

Illustrated by Carole Byard, Written by Faith Ringgold
1992 Illustrator Award Winner

About the Book

Eight-year-old Cassie lives in New York City in Harlem where she lets her imagination soar as the family spends summer evenings on the roof top of their apartment building. In her mind she flies through the sky over the George Washington Bridge (which she claims as her own), and dreams of being rich some day. She tells of her dad who works on steel girders in tall buildings and wants to be a union member. She knows this can't be because his father was not a union member. In Cassie's dream world, her mother can sleep late and there will be ice cream for dessert every night. These are her dreams as she makes her nightly flight over "Tar Beach." *(Crown, 1991. 32 pp. Reading Level: 2.5)*

About the Author/Artist

Faith Ringgold has long had a fascination with quilts. She began her career as an artist over 35 years ago and is widely known today for her painted story quilts which combine painting, quilted fabrics and storytelling. Her work can be found in many of the world's famous art collections including the Metropolitan Museum of Art and The Museum of Modern Art. In addition to *Tar Beach*, her other children's books include: *Aunt Harriet's Underground Railroad in the Sky; Bonjour, Lonnie; Dinner at Aunt Connie's House;* and *My Dream of Martin Luther King.*

Before Reading Activity

Ranking

Form small groups and have each rank order the following summer activities, starting with what they would want to do most. Choose one person in each group to tell the reasons for their first and last choices.

1. Go swimming.

2. Fly over a city.

3. Eat ice cream.

4. Play a board game.

5. Eat supper on a rooftop.

After Reading Activities

Questions to Think About

1. Is using your imagination a good thing? Why or why not?

2. How would this story change if Cassie lived in the country?

3. How are the tall buildings and the bridge Cassie sees alike?

4. What injustices did you see in the story? (What wasn't fair?)

5. What sights might Cassie see if she flew during the day rather than at night?

6. What was Cassie's favorite sight? Why do you think so?

7. How many other ways might Cassie have traveled around her neighborhood?

8. Cassie said "It's easy. Anyone can fly." Do you agree? Why or why not?

Imaginative Apples

Create imaginative apples and carefully write in the tissue paper windows sights Cassie would see in New York City, which is often called "The Big Apple."

For this activity you will need: black construction paper; red, yellow or green tissue paper; black thread; scissors; pencils; and glue.

Directions

1. Cut two apple outlines from black construction paper.

2. Cut a single sheet of tissue paper to fit between black construction paper frame.

3. Glue the two pieces of black construction paper together with the tissue paper between them.

4. Hang apples with black thread. Hang where light will best show through them.

A Newspaper Game

Divide the group into teams of four members each. Each group receives a news-paper. This does not have to be a current newspaper. Each team also receives this list of items to find. Items can be cut out or torn out and placed in order in a pile. The team finding the most items within a given time period is the winner.

Find

1. A picture of an apple or the word "apple."

2. A picture of a tall building.

3. A picture or an article about a bridge.

4. A recipe or an ad that mentions ice cream.

5. A picture of some type of city transportation.

6. A picture or article about an apartment house.

7. Cut out letters that spell the word "imagination."

8. A picture or article of or about a policeman.

9. The name of the mayor of a city.

10. The name of a city located on a river.

11. A picture or name of a building owned by a city.

12. A picture of a bird you'd most likely find in a city.

An Internet Activity

Have the children create their own tales. A worksheet for this activity can be found on page 91.

Additional Reading

Stories of the City

Isadora, Rachel. *City Seen from A to Z.* Morrow, 1992. 32 pp. RL: 1.0. The diversity and hear of New York City are shown from A to Z.

Wong, Olive. *From My Window.* Silver Burdett, 1995. 32 pp. RL: 1.0. An African American boy observes the city on a snowy day.

Hector-Smalls, Irene. *Jonathan and His Mommy.* LittleBrown, 1992. 32 pp. RL: 1.0. Jonathan and his mother explore their urban neighborhood with a series if steps going from crazy criss-cross to reggae.

Wyeth, Sharon. *Something Beautiful.* Doubleday, 1998. 32 pp. RL: 2.0. A little girl looks for beauty in everyday sights in her city neighborhood.

Littlesugar, Amy. Illus. by Floyd Cooper. *Tree of Hope.* Philomel, 1999. 32 pp. RL: 3.0. Florrie's daddy had been an actor before the depression hit and the theater was closed. But she and her daddy often wished on the Tree of Hope that stood just outside the theater entrance. And her wish came true in an unexpected way.

Internet Activity

Visit the following website to create some wacky tales. Or, read tales created by others.

Wacky Web Tales
http://www.eduplace.com/tales/index.html

Now create your own Tall City Tale. Follow the directions below to create your own tall city tale.

Think of a word for each of these items.

1. a size
2. a color
3. an animal
4. a place to sleep
5. way to travel
6. something to read
7. same as number 3
8. animal sound
9. an action word that ends in "ing"
10. an exclamation
11. unusual place

Use the words in place of the numbers below.

Beside the (1) (2) Empire State Building there was a (3) who was sound asleep on a (4). A policeman approached on a (5). The policeman was was reading a (6) and stumbled over the (7) who awakened and gave a loud (8) that frightened the passersby when they saw it (9). (10) the policeman yelled and chased it into a (11) where it was never seen again.

Read your fantasy city tall tale aloud.

Coretta Scott King Award & Honor Books

Prior to 1974, the CSK Award was given to authors only.

1970 *Martin Luther King, Jr.: Man of Peace* Lillie Patterson (Garrard)

1971 *Black Troubador: Langston Hughes* Charlemae Rollins (Rand McNally)

1972 *17 Black Artists* Elton C. Fax (Dodd)

1973 *I Never Had It Made: The Autobiography of Jackie Robinson* as told to Alfred Duckett (Putnam)

1974 **Author Award:** *Ray Charles* Sharon Bell Mathis (Crowell)

Illustrator Award: *Ray Charles* ill. by George Ford, text by Sharon Bell Mathis (Crowell)

1975 **Author Award:** *The Legend of Africana* Dorothy Robinson (Johnson Publishing)

Illustrator Award: No award given.

1976 **Author Award:** *Duey's Tale* Pearl Bailey (Harcourt)

Illustrator Award: No award given.

1977 **Author Award:** *The Story of Stevie Wonder* James Haskins (Lothrop)

Illustrator Award: No award given.

1978 **Author Award:** *Africa Dream* Eloise Greenfield (Crowell)
Honor Books: *The Days When the Animals Talked: Black Folk Tales and How They Came to Be* William J. Faulkner (Follett)
Marvin and Tige Frankcina Glass (St. Martin's)
Mary McCleod Bethune Eloise Greenfield (Crowell)
Barbara Jordan James Haskins (Dial)
Coretta Scott King Lillie Patterson (Garrard)
Portia: The Life of Portia Washington Pittman, the Daughter of Booker T. Washington Ruth Ann Stewart (Doubleday)

Illustrator Award: *Africa Dream* ill. by Carole Bayard, text by Eloise Greenfield (Crowell)

1979 **Author Award:** *Escape to Freedom* Ossie Davis (Viking)
Honor Books: *Benjamin Banneker* Lillie Patterson (Abingdon)
I Have a Sister, My Sister Is Deaf Jeanne Peterson (Harper)
Justice and Her Brothers Virginia Hamilton (Greenwillow)
Skates of Uncle Richard Carol Fenner (Random)

Illustrator Award: *Something on My Mind* ill. by Tom Feelings, text by Nikki Grimes (Dial)

1980 **Author Award:** *The Young Landlords* Walter Dean Myers (Viking)
Honor Books: *Movin' Up* Berry Gordy (Harper)
Childtimes: A Three-Generation Memoir Eloise Greenfield and Lessie Jones Little (Harper)
Andrew Young: Young Man with a Mission James Haskins (Lothrop)
James Van Der Zee: The Picture Takin' Man James Haskins (Dodd)
Let the Lion Eat Straw Ellease Southerland (Scribner)

Illustrator Award: *Cornrows* ill. by Carole Byard, text by Camille Yarborough (Coward-McCann)

1981 **Author Award:** *This Life* Sidney Poitier (Knopf)
Honor Book: *Don't Explain: A Song of Billie Holiday* Alexis De Veaux (Harper)

Illustrator Award: *Beat the Story Drum, Pum-Pum* ill. and text by Ashley Bryan (Atheneum)
Honor Books: *Grandmama's Joy* ill. by Carole Byard, text by Eloise Greenfield (Collins)
Count on Your Fingers African Style ill. by Jerry Pinkney, text by Claudia Zaslavsky (Crowell)

1982 **Author Award:** *Let the Circle Be Unbroken* Mildred D. Taylor (Dial)
Honor Books: *Rainbow Jordan* Alice Childress (Coward-McCann)
Lou in the Limelight Kristin Hunter (Scribner)
Mary: An Autobiography Mary E. Mebane (Viking)

Illustrator Award: *Mother Crocodile; An Uncle Amadou Tale from Sengal* ill. by John Steptoe, text by Rosa Guy (Delacorte)
Honor Book: *Daydreamers* ill. by Tom Feelings, text by Eloise Greenfield (Dial)

1983 **Author Award:** *Sweet Whispers, Brother Rush* Virginia Hamilton (Philomel)
Honor Book: *This Strange New Feeling* Julius Lester (Dial)

Illustrator Award: *Black Child* ill. and text by Peter Mugabane (Knopf)
Honor Books: *All the Colors of the Race* ill. by John Steptoe, text by Arnold Adoff (Lothrop)
I'm Going to Sing: Black American Spirituals ill. by Ashley Bryan (Atheneum)
Just Us Women ill. by Pat Cummings, text by Jeanette Caines (Harper)

1984 Author Award: *Everett Anderson's Good-bye* Lucille Clifton (Holt)
Special Citation: *The Words of Martin Luther King, Jr.* Coretta Scott King, comp. (Newmarket Press)
Honor Books: *The Magical Adventures of Pretty Pearl* Virginia Hamilton (Harper)
Lena Horne James Haskins (Coward-McCann)
Bright Shadow Joyce Carol Thomas (Avon)
Because We Are Mildred Pitts Walter

Illustrator Award: *My Mama Needs Me* ill. by Pat Cummings, text by Mildred Pitts Walter (Lothrop)

1985 Author Award: *Motown and Didi* Walter Dean Myers (Viking)
Honor Books: *Circle of Gold* Candy Dawson Boyd (Apple/Scholastic)
A Little Love Virginia Hamilton (Philomel)

Illustrator Award: No award given.

1986 Author Award: *The People Could Fly: American Black Folktales* Virginia Hamilton (Knopf)
Honor Books: *Junius Over Far* Virginia Hamilton (Harper)
Trouble's Child Mildred Pitts Walter (Lothrop)

Illustrator Award: *The Patchwork Quilt* ill. by Jerry Pinkney, text by Valerie Flournoy (Dial)
Honor Book: *The People Could Fly: American Black Folktales* ill. by Leo and Diane Dillon, text by Virginia Hamilton (Knopf)

1987 Author Award: *Justin and the Best Biscuits in the World* Mildred Pitts Walter (Lothrop)
Honor Books: *Lion and the Ostrich Chicks and Other African Folk Tales* Ashley Bryan (Atheneum)
Which Way Freedom Joyce Hansen (Walker)

Illustrator Award: *Half a Moon and One Whole Star* ill. by Jerry Pinkney, text by Crescent Dragonwagon (Macmillan)
Honor Books: *Lion and the Ostrich Chicks and Other African Folk Tales* ill. and text by Ashley Bryan (Atheneum)
C.L.O.U.D.S. Pat Cummings (Lothrop)

1988 Author Award: *The Friendship* Mildred L. Taylor (Dial)
Honor Books: *An Enchanted Hair Tale* Alexis De Veaux (Harper)
The Tales of Uncle Remus: The Adventures of Brer Rabbit Julius Lester (Dial)

Illustrator Award: *Mufaro's Beautiful Daughters: An African Tale* ill. and text by John Steptoe (Lothrop)
Honor Books: *What a Morning! The Christmas Story in*

Black Spirituals ill. by Ashley Bryan, selected by John Langstaff (Macmillan)
The Invisible Hunters: A Legend from the Miskito Indians of Nicaragua ill. by Joe Sam, compiled by Harriet Rohmer, et al (Children's Press)

1989 Author Award: *Fallen Angels* Walter Dean Myers (Scholastic)
Honor Books: *A Thief in the Village and Other Stories* James Berry (Orchard)
Anthony Burns: The Defeat and Triumph of a Fugitive Slave Virginia Hamilton (Knopf)

Illustrator Award: *Mirandy and Brother Wind* ill. by Jerry Pinkney, text by Patricia McKissack (Knopf)
Honor Books: *Under the Sunday Tree* ill. by Amos Ferguson, text by Eloise Greenfield (Harper)
Storm in the Night ill. by Pat Cummings, text by Mary Stolz (Harper)

1990 Author Award: *A Long Hard Journey: The Story of the Pullman Porter* Patricia C. & Frederick L. McKissack (Walker)
Honor Books: *Nathaniel Talking* Eloise Greenfield (Black Butterfly)
The Bells of Christmas Virginia Hamilton (Harcourt)
Martin Luther King, Jr. and the Freedom Movement Lillie Patterson (Facts on File)

Illustrator Award: *Nathaniel Talking* ill. by Jan Spivey Gilchrist, text by Eloise Greenfield (Black Butterfly)
Honor Book: *The Talking Eggs* ill. by Jerry Pinkney, text by Robert San Souci (Dial)

1991 Author Award: *The Road to Memphis* Mildred D. Taylor (Dial)
Honor Books: *Black Dance in America* James Haskins (Crowell)
When I Am Old With You Angela Johnson (Orchard)

Illustrator Award: *Aida* ill. by Leo and Diane Dillon, text by Leontyne Price (Harcourt)

1992 Author Award: *Now Is Your Time: The African American Struggle for Freedom* Walter Dean Myers (HarperCollins)
Honor Book: *Night on Neighborhood Street* Eloise Greenfield (Dial)

Illustrator Award: *Tar Beach* ill. and text by Faith Ringgold (Crown)
Honor Books: *All Night, All Day: A Child's First Book of African American Spirituals* Illustrated and selected by Ashley Bryan (Atheneum)
Night on Neighborhood Street ill. by Jan Spivey Gilchrist, text by Eloise Greenfield (Dial)

1993 Author Award: *The Dark Thirty: Southern Tales of the Supernatural* Patricia A. McKissack (Knopf)
Honor Books: *Mississippi Challenge* Mildred Pitts Walter (Bradbury)
Sojourner Truth: Ain't I a Woman? Patricia C. & Frederick L. McKissack (Scholastic)
Somewhere in the Darkness Walter Dean Myers (Scholastic)

Illustrator Award: *The Origin of Life on Earth: An African Creation Myth* ill. by Kathleen Atkins Wilson, retold by David A. Anderson/SANKOFA (Sights)
Honor Books: *Little Eight John* ill. by Wil Clay, text by Jan Wahl (Lodestar)
Sukey and the Mermaid ill. by Brian Pinkney, text by Robert San Souci (Four Winds)
Working Cotton ill. by Carole Byard, text by Sherley Anne Williams (Harcourt)

1994 Author Award: *Toning the Sweep* Angela Johnson (Orchard)
Honor Books: *Brown Honey in Broom Wheat Tea* Joyce Carol Thomas (HarperCollins)
Malcolm X: By Any Means Necessary Walter Dean Myers (Scholastic)

Illustrator Award: *Soul Looks Back in Wonder* ill. by Tom Feelings, text ed. by Phyllis Fogelman (Dial Books for Young Readers)
Honor Books: *Brown Honey in Broom Wheat Tea* ill. by Floyd Cooper, text by Joyce Carol Thomas (HarperCollins)
Uncle Jed's Barbershop ill. by James Ransome, text by Margaree King Mitchell (Simon & Schuster)

1995 Author Award: *Christmas in the Big House, Christmas in the Quarters* Patricia C. & Frederick L. McKissack (Scholastic)
Honor Books: *The Captive* Joyce Hansen (Scholastic)
I Hadn't Meant to Tell You This Jacqueline Woodson (Delacorte)
Black Diamond: Story of the Negro Baseball League Patricia C. & Frederick L. McKissack (Scholastic)

Illustrator Award: *The Creation* ill. by James Ransome, text by James Weldon Johnson (Holiday House)
Honor Books: *The Singing Man* ill. by Terea Shaffer, text by Angela Shelf Medearis (Holiday House)
Meet Danitra Brown ill. by Floyd Cooper, text by Nikki Grimes (Lothrop, Lee & Shepard)

1996 Author Award: *Her Stories* Virginia Hamilton (Scholastic/Blue Sky Press)
Honor Books: *The Watsons Go to Birmingham–1963* Christopher Paul Curtis (Delacorte)
Like Sisters on the Homefront Rita Williams-Garcia (Delacorte)
From the Notebooks of Melanin Sun Jacqueline Woodson (Scholastic/Blue Sky Press)

Illustrator Award: *The Middle Passage: White Ships Black Cargo* Illustrations and text by Tom Feelings (Dial Books for Young Readers)
Honor Books: *Her Stories* ill. by Leo and Diane Dillon, text by Virginia Hamilton (Scholastic/ Blue Sky Press)
The Faithful Friend ill. by Brian Pinkney, text by Robert San Souci (Simon & Schuster Books for Young Readers)

1997 Author Award: *Slam* Walter Dean Myers (Scholastic)
Honor Book: *Rebels against Slavery: American Slave Revolts* Patricia C. & Frederick L. McKissack (Scholastic)

Illustrator Award: *Minty: A Story of Young Harriet Tubman* ill. by Jerry Pinkney, text by Alan Schroeder (Dial Books for Young Readers)
Honor Books: *The Palm of My Heart: Poetry by African American Children* ill. by Gregorie Christie, ed. by Davida Adedjouma (Lee & Low)
Running the Road to ABC ill. by Reynold Ruffins, text by Denize Lauture (Simon & Schuster Books for Young Readers)
Neeny Coming, Neeny Going ill. by Synthia Saint James, text by Karen English (BridgeWater Books)

1998 Author Award: *Forged by Fire* Sharon M. Draper (Atheneum)
Honor Books: *Bayard Rustin: Behind the Scenes of the Civil Rights Movement* James Haskins (Hyperion)
I Thought My Soul Would Rise and Fly: The Diary of Patsy, a Freed Girl Joyce Hansen (Scholastic)

Illustrator Award: *In Daddy's Arms I am Tall: African Americans Celebrating Fathers* ill. by Javaka Steptoe, text by Alan Schroeder (Lee & Low) **Honor Books:** *Ashley Bryan's ABC of African American Poetry* Illus./text by Ashley Bryan (Jean Karl/Atheneum)
Harlem ill. by Christopher Myers, text by Walter Dean Myers (Scholastic)
The Hunterman and the Crocodile Illustrations and text by Baba Wagué Diakité (Scholastic)

1999 Author Award: *Heaven* Angela Johnson (Simon & Schuster)
Honor Book: *Jazmin's Notebook* Nikki Grimes (Dial)
Breaking Ground, Breaking Silence: The Story of New York's African Burial Ground Joyce Hansen and Gary McGowan (Henry Holt)
The Other Side: Shorter Poems Angela Johnson (Orchard)

Illustrator Award: *i see the rhythm* ill. by Michele Wood, text by Toyomi Igus (Children's Book Press)
Honor Books: *I Have Heard of a Land* ill. by Floyd Cooper, text by Joyce Carol Thomas (Joanna Cotler Books/HarperCollins)
The Bat Boy and His Violin ill. by E.B. Lewis, text by Gavin Curtis (Simon & Schuster)
Duke Ellington: The Piano Prince and His Orchestra ill. by Brian Pinkney, text by Andrea Davis Pinkney (Hyperion Books for Children)

2000 Author Award: *Bud, Not Buddy* Christopher Paul Curtis (Delacorte)
Honor Books: *Francie* Karen English (Farrar, Straus & Giroux)
Black Hands, White Sails: The Story of African-American Whalers Patricia C. and Frederick L. McKissack (Scholastic)
Monster Walter Dean Myers (HarperCollins)

Illustrator Award: *In the Time of the Drums* ill. by Brian Pinkney, text by Kim L. Siegelson (Jump at the Sun/Hyperion Books for Children)
Honor Books: *My Rows and Piles of Coins* ill. by E. B. Lewis, text by Tololwa M. Mollel (Clarion)
Black Cat ill. and text by Christopher Myers (Scholastic)